Challenges in Counselling: Student Counselling

Challenges in Counselling: Student Counselling

Kirsten Amis

Orders: please contact Bookpoint Ltd, 130 Milton Park, Abingdon, Oxon OX14 4SB. Telephone: (44) 01235 827720. Fax: (44) 01235 400454. Lines are open from 9.00 - 5.00, Monday to Saturday, with a 24 hour message answering service. You can also order through our website www.hoddereducation.co.uk

If you have any comments to make about this, or any of our other titles, please send them to educationenquiries@hodder.co.uk

British Library Cataloguing in Publication Data

A catalogue record for this title is available from the British Library

ISBN: 978 1 444 1 8775 5

Published 2013

Impression number   10 9 8 7 6 5 4 3 2 1

Year   2016 2015 2014 2013

Cover photo © Andres Rodriguez – Fotolia.com

Typeset by Datapage (India) Pvt. Ltd.

Printed and bound by CPI Group (UK) Ltd., Croydon, CR0 4YY for Hodder Education, an Hachette UK Company, 338 Euston Road, London, NW1 3BH.

Contents

Foreword   vii

About the author   ix

Acknowledgements   x

1 Introduction   1

2 Settings   15

3 Theory and skills   25

4 Identifying anxieties   45

5 Strategies   59

6 Possible impact on clients   79

7 Professional issues   91

8 Ethical issues   101

9 Research   119

List of abbreviations   133

Appendix   139

Index   145

Foreword

For the past 17 years I have been a lecturer in counselling based in a Further Education college but over the past few years I have found myself sliding into the informal role of manager/coordinator of the student counselling service. I had been counselling students within a Student Services department since 2000, so I felt quite comfortable accepting the role. However, my experience has led me to discover that although there is a plethora of interesting, informative and helpful literature out there to help guide and shape a counselling service, it can be elusive. I felt that having a range of basic information in one source would make life easier for the counsellor working with adults in an educational establishment. By this, I mean providing structured counselling sessions to students over the age of 18 studying in universities, colleges, through distance learning and in community-based settings. By its very nature there are bound to be overlaps in this area; for example, we work with school-leavers who are under 18 which is very common in Further Education. I have tried to balance this focus on our work with an awareness of external pressures that often shape our provision. These can include government recommendations, funding council requirements and the measurement of outcomes to justify our very existence but as most of these are based on legislation they are prone to change frequently which must be demonstrated in our reflexivity.

I am also aware that many staff working as counsellors within educational counselling services are not in paid employment but are volunteering to gain client hours as they work towards their professional accreditation, and many are students on placement fulfilling a requirement of their course.

This book will hopefully be of use to anyone working within the area, and I don't apologise for some of the content being very basic. When facing challenges and difficulties in a work setting, we often just want a straightforward and easy-to-understand text before we search for one that focuses on a particular area in greater depth. When asking student counsellors who are on placement with us for their thoughts, there was an overwhelmingly clear response: it is not easy to find relevant material if you are not already a member of a professional organisation. Therefore, I have aimed to pull together a collection of information that addresses challenges a new counsellor might have when starting to work with adult students.

I hope this text provides some of the answers or sources of information that you might be searching for at times of stress and highlights some of the issues and hurdles we face on a regular basis when working within this stimulating, challenging and lively environment.

Kirsten Amis
March 2013

About the author

Kirsten Amis is a counselling lecturer at a college in Glasgow where she also manages the student counselling service. She has twenty years of counselling experience within NHS, voluntary and private practice environments, and experience working with addictive behaviours. Kirsten is a Scottish Qualifications Authority Qualification Development Specialist and External Verifier for counselling and is also a clinical supervisor for two addiction services. She is currently the BACP: Universities & Colleges Four Nations Representative for Scotland.

Acknowledgements

This book would not exist without the patient encouragement and support of Ruben Hale, Stephen Halder and Matthew Sullivan at Hodder Education and the valuable and enlightening contributions by Jane, Elaine, Heidi, Judy and John (you know who you are!). Great thanks must also go to Ian MacMillan for the passion and care he invested into his intricate doodles and to Mum, Jeff and Conrad for being as quietly supportive as ever. Finally, to Andy for his patience, tolerance, eagle-eyes and cups of 'camomile infusion'. I can't believe he didn't raise his eyes, tut loudly and say 'Here we go again'!

Chapter 1
Introduction

The context of this book

Working as a counsellor and supporting adult students brings with it some very specific issues. It might sound negative to start with what this book is not, but it is written explicitly for counsellors who are supporting adults and adolescents in education environments and therefore it does not include working with children. There is already an assortment of very specific literature available for working therapeutically with children and young people in schools.

Now for what this book does cover. The themes within this book focus on potential challenges and difficulties that a counsellor might encounter during their working day. The content and focus are very much influenced by my own personal experiences and those of colleagues throughout the UK during my time working in this area. Managing the counselling service is a role that I find deeply rewarding, although of course, I have happened across a range of challenging situations over the years, many of which have found their way on to these pages. To provide a more rounded picture, I have invited other counsellors working in this area, both employed (paid and volunteering) and on student placements to contribute their experiences and I do hope their perspectives are interesting and useful.

For the sake of clarity, there are some instances where I shall refer to the student as the 'client' if it is in the context of a counselling session. When discussing theory and experiences in general, I shall simply stick with 'student'. I hope this is not interpreted as negative labelling but rather to identify with an individual as well as their role.

This first chapter will be focusing on the role of the counselling service, how counsellors currently working in the sector feel about their experiences, and common difficulties that crop up, one of which can be the complex array of jargon, acronyms and technical terms bandied about in education. Chapter 2 develops this further to consider specific anxieties and challenges that counsellors can encounter. These can include financial constraints, practical issues and the pressure of being caught between the very different goals of, on the one hand, supporting students in a flexible, therapeutic and reflexive manner and on the other, having to demonstrate the ability to manage time, budgeting and measure outcomes. In Chapter 3 we consider the similarities, differences, strengths and weaknesses that we might experience when working within a range of different settings such as universities, colleges, distance learning courses and community-based campuses. Many of the issues already raised will be considered in Chapter 4 where we move on to identifying strategies for successful and efficacious working practices and reflect on how we might manage some of our challenges. These can be influenced by and link in with professional issues such as accreditation, employment, complaints and supervision that will be examined in Chapter 5. Although this is a book intended for readers who are already working in counselling or who are currently studying counselling, Chapter 6 will examine some of the major theories and skills we work with in the context of education. By this I mean that we will not be covering the theories at a basic level, but rather view them through the framework of application, identifying the main uses and what they might mean to us in the therapeutic process. We will focus on our clients in Chapter 7 where the role of student and the impact that aspects such as age, studying and possibly living away from home for the first time can have on the counselling relationship. In Chapter 8 we will move on to ethical issues and consider the balance we must achieve between our standards of professionalism, meeting the needs of the client and being aware of legislation, policies and guidelines surrounding boundaries and the law. The importance and influence of research will be examined in Chapter 9 where we will consider the possible implications of past and current studies and reflect on what their findings tell us about working in this field. Finally, at the end of the book is a List of Abbreviations which will explain some of the language particular to this area of counselling (acronyms in the List are in **bold** throughout the book). It also contains an Appendix showing a categorisation system recommended for recording and monitoring issues that clients present us with.

The settings

The four settings that we will be considering can vary greatly in their size, provision, structure and ethos. The lack of continuity across the sector has been evident for many years although it is only fair to acknowledge that there are instances when this lack of uniformity can be advantageous, especially if it allows for flexibility in meeting the needs of the establishment. This issue has long been acknowledged and there are several UK-wide working groups in place to increase the continuity of support for those in education. One of these is the **Universities UK**/GuildHE Working Group for the Promotion of Mental Well-Being in Higher Education (**MWBHE**), which has the following three aims:

- Promote collaboration between the different sectors, agencies and professional groups with responsibility for mental wellbeing in Higher Education
- Be a reference point for government bodies, managers in the NHS and educational institutions and practitioners in respect of mental wellbeing in Higher Education
- Influence policy on issues related to mental wellbeing in Higher Education.

We can see from this that the MWBHE has a fairly wide remit and focus on collaborative working to bring professionals from differing areas together with the shared aim of supporting the mental wellbeing of Higher Education students. The British Association for Counselling and Psychotherapy (**BACP**) underpins a similar division named the Association for University and College Counselling (**BACP: U&C**), which produces and publishes a wide range of helpful material that is regularly updated to ensure it is current. It aims to:

- Represent counsellors in Higher Education (**HE**) and Further Education (**FE**) through our committees and special interest groups
- Offer professional support through our advisory service, journal, research, conference and mail bases
- Promote the integration of counselling services into HE and FE institutions, offering advice and best practice guidelines.

As a member of the **AUCC** I refer to their fact sheets and professional guidance often and have found them invaluable in the development of the policies and procedures for our college counselling service. Because of this, I have referred to them regularly throughout this text.

To highlight mental health issues from the student perspective, the National Union of Students (**NUS**) runs a mental health campaign called Think Positive, which is designed to challenge the stigma and negative assumptions made about mental illness. Similar to the **MWBHE** and **BACP: U&C**, it is involved in seeking information about students' mental wellbeing, monitoring its prevalence and the support mechanisms that are in place as well as being involved at a national level to consult on policy-making. In 'Sharing Practice in Mental Health Improvement' (2010), Yaqoob identified the aims and objectives of the initiative as being:

- To tackle the issue of mental health stigma in the student population across Scotland, and
- To work with students' associations to create local anti-stigma campaigns, train students in mental health first aid, and further research the issue of mental health in the student population.

Although this research was funded by the Scottish Government and the participants were Scottish students, the findings are widely representative with many recognised themes regarding mental wellbeing and is therefore applicable throughout the UK. How we consider these themes is bound to be influenced by the environment we are working within and the context that this provides.

Universities

The first setting we will touch on is the University or Higher Education sector. Essentially, universities deliver academic courses at undergraduate and postgraduate level so offer HE certificates and HE diplomas as well as degrees and higher degrees. This means that students will be working towards an award at level 4 or above in the Framework for Higher Education Qualifications in England, Wales and Northern Ireland (**FHEQ**) or level 7 and above in the Scottish Credit Qualifications Framework (**SCQF**). Although this levelling of courses might initially sound confusing, it is actually quite straightforward and the qualification frameworks are included at the end of the book. In addition to a difference in range of qualifications on offer, universities tend to have a considerably larger student population than other education settings, with some resembling a small town. Having this larger student base incrementally increases the number of students potentially accessing the counselling service. There is a significant level of collaborative working with university staff liaising with NHS services to ensure they support students in a manner that is consistent with the care they are receiving elsewhere. Counselling services are often based in student health centres as part of a more holistic approach to provision. This is one of the many reasons why university counselling services tend to be not just very busy numbers-wise but also employ a larger support team. Being such a growth area has seen the quantity of universities in the UK rise, the diversity of student populations grow, the numbers of international students has increased and the expansion in the range of available subject areas make counselling in an HE setting more challenging than ever before.

Colleges

Compared to universities, FE colleges tend to have an even more disparate approach to supporting students' mental wellbeing with, according to the AUCC 2006–7 report, some not providing any in-house counselling at all but relying on referring students to external agencies. I was interested in how these colleges supported their students' mental health so contacted several to find out their procedure. It was explained to me that they do this via referral, mainly to the student's GP with the student's consent. It is difficult not to generalise here but even large colleges who have a well-developed and structured counselling service tend not to employ the number of counsellors that universities do. Again, referring to the BACP: U&C study, colleges often employ just one or two counsellors and 50 per cent of respondents reported having no administrative staff. It appears that because colleges are usually, but not always, smaller than universities the counselling departments reflect this in that they are often smaller and employ fewer people. Admittedly, on average they are supporting a smaller student base but it can be isolating and stressful to be working on your own or as part of a very small team. There seems to be less recognition of counselling in colleges as the service is often tagged onto Student Services rather than being viewed as a discrete department.

Community-based education

Many universities and colleges have more than one campus (often referred to as satellite, external or community campuses). Whether counselling is available or not on site depends upon the size of the facility and the ethos of the organisation. Larger institutions are more likely to have counsellors working in more than one site but this is not always feasible in smaller settings, especially if there is only a lone practitioner to cover the whole institution. Our college currently has four sites and although counselling is only available in the main campus, we try to reinforce that the counselling service is there for all through marketing (posters on the back of toilet doors, links on the website and counsellors visiting classes at the beginning of term to introduce themselves). Despite this, we have not had a single community-based student make an appointment, but there are possible reasons for that. These can include some major constraints such as access, transport, being in a different building or simply not being aware of the service in the first place. Because of this, I have spent time talking to students studying in the community and was surprised at how high a percentage were already accessing counselling through their GP, local addiction centre or voluntary organisation. Studies have demonstrated that community-based students can be quite vulnerable (Gallacher *et al*, 2000 and 2002) but I felt this was reinforced during my meetings and discussions.

Distance learning

Last but certainly not least is distance learning courses where students enrol, study and submit assessments online with minimum or no contact with a centre. The fact that there is every possibility that tutor, student and class members may never meet can lead to significant feelings of isolation, particularly if the individual is not a confident learner or has been out of education for any length of time. The method of support offered within this setting can vary depending upon the institution. On most courses, students are provided with contact details for a course or personal tutor with whom they are encouraged to discuss issues that relate directly to their learning. The tutor is then able to refer them for additional support if the relevant service is available. Larger education establishments may offer centralised services such as counselling but tend to focus more on other methods of focused learning support because of the possible distances involved.

The role of a counselling service

Currently there is no single model adopted for setting up and managing a counselling service within an educational establishment. This slightly disjointed approach has resulted in a lack of continuity between colleges and universities when developing policies and procedures and managing their services to support students' wellbeing. This was very clearly highlighted in the BACP: U&E national research into student counselling service provision in FE throughout the UK in 2006–7, which emphasised just how diverse colleges in particular are. I am surprised that there is such a wide spectrum of service provision with a small yet significant number of establishments not offering any in-house counselling at all, despite research acknowledging the positive role of counselling in the success and retention of students (for example, BACP, 2012). However to help guide those managing and working within a student counselling service, the BACP: U&C has published a guide covering the purpose of such a service, the counselling activities undertaken and working structures required to maintain good practice (BACP, 2010). Of course it can be argued that each establishment has its own specific issues and method of management so a level of flexibility can be a very positive aspect. What we do find is that universities tend to have more formally structured counselling services, probably because they have a far larger student population on average and there is often funding streams available to allow for employing paid counsellors. Colleges tend to range from no counselling service to a highly structured and integrated department. Counselling provision in external campuses and satellite community campuses tends to depend very much on the size of the campus or student population and as with all settings, funding. Students studying via distance learning have an even more disparate experience with some organisations providing therapeutic support via Skype, telephone or the internet, and others not having any support mechanisms in place.

There are many tasks involved in the smooth running of an educational counselling service, some of which are included here:

- Managing the application process, interviewing, appointment and ongoing support of counsellors.
- Ensuring all counsellors receive regular external counselling supervision (either provided by the service or the counsellor takes responsibility for their own)
- Monitoring and supporting the counsellors
- Collating a comprehensive set of statistics to monitor the overall effectiveness of the service
- Liaising with external agencies (such as securing student placements)
- Processing and/or liaising with social workers, the NHS, GPs, court referrals, etc.
- Prompt crisis intervention for students experiencing immediate difficulties (for example, a suicide attempt, panic attack or even physical fighting)
- Developing and updating all documentation for counsellors
- Maintaining the professionalism and high standard of the service to meet the needs of the university or college
- Conducting counselling sessions with students
- Regular meetings with staff (service administrator, student support services, management)
- Developing relevant policies and procedures in keeping with current legislation and institution guidelines

- Monitoring and adhering to national standards, for example, mental health targets
- Supporting under-24-year-olds in line with government youth employment strategies, for example, Opportunities for All, Skills Development Scotland, Certificate for Work Readiness
- Working in partnership with external agencies to provide specific support for affected students.

Of course there are many more tasks involved that will differ from service to service depending upon the remit of the department. As well as considering the possible work and structure of services, we must not forget the perceptions and understanding of those already employed as counsellors.

Figure 1.1 Students in crisis

Experiences of counsellors

I felt it might be of use to hear from counsellors who have been working in this area to paint a picture of their experiences. Throughout the book we shall hear from several counsellors who have contributed: Jane and Judy, counsellors within **FE** colleges; Elaine, a volunteer counsellor working towards her **BACP** accreditation; Heidi, a student placement and John, counselling in a university. Their feedback is mainly positive although they have raised some challenges they have faced. Elaine's first three years were spent as on student placement with her fourth year volunteering. She highlights the sense of satisfaction she gains when a student is successful in their course and the impact that coordinated support can have on that outcome:

Voices

Elaine

'During my four years working as a college counsellor I have worked with a diverse and broad client base. These amazing individuals have given me a deep-rooted belief in the person-centred approach to counselling; it works, I have witnessed it through my successful journey with my clients. Countless times near the end of the therapeutic relationship it has been disclosed to me that without the access to counselling, the client would never have reached the end of their course. I believe this is proof that an academic and structured organization such as a college can work in unison with a counselling body to provide a student with structured learning and emotional support to get qualifications.'

Judy, on the other hand, is employed as a counsellor and has been for many years. Her feedback draws attention to specific areas of her work that she finds both positive and negative and how she deals with it:

Voices

Judy

'I have been employed as a college counsellor for many years and have always found it to balance between frustrating and rewarding. I find the level of DNAs [those who did not attend] higher than in private practice but far lower than that of the charity I work for. In my experience it has been younger students who have attended more than mature students, although I haven't read anything into that simply because statistically, there are more students under the age of 24 at the college. I do find that I am affected by the impact that poor parenting has on them which is an ongoing theme for me in supervision. I always attend group supervision as it's a compulsory part of the role. Sometimes I'm the only counsellor working so I can feel quite isolated but group supervision allows me to meet up with the rest of the team. I mainly use the sessions for support but also as a type of monitoring; it puts my mind at rest when I hear similar issues being raised by my colleagues.'

Here, Heidi, a student placement, talks of feeling supported when receiving counselling as a student and of the flexibility working in this sector afforded her:

Voices

Heidi

'I have had both the experience of being counselled and of counselling students within an adult education setting. My experience of being counselled was very positive. I found the system easy to use with high-quality counselling and no waiting list. I was able to find a time that suited me between my lectures and received enough support to enable me to continue with my course when I had felt overwhelmed and had considered leaving due to personal issues. My experience of counselling students within higher education has also been very positive. I was given the freedom to work using the approach I was training in with the opportunity for group supervision if I so wished. Both colleges I have worked in provided me with appointments and kept in touch if there were any cancellations.'

Common challenges

Although we can never guess which students might engage with the counselling service, we do know that they come with their own unique issues that they will process in their own way. One of the most interesting aspects of working within this area is that the age range of students we can find ourselves working with is enormous extending from recent school leavers who are still developing from children into adults, through the spectrum to experienced and mature students with considerable life experience. This makes working as a counsellor in colleges and universities somewhat similar to working as a counsellor in many other settings. However, the common theme that runs through all clients is that they are engaged in some way with education. Their motivation, interest, attendance, ability and level of engagement may well differ but they are still matriculated on to a course. One of the major differences between students in schools and students in adult education settings is that it is compulsory for the former to attend but for the latter, the majority have exercised an element of choice in their studies. Admittedly courses for continuing professional development (**CPD**), employment-related training or modern apprenticeships may sit somewhere between the two, but adult learners are often able to establish links between the potential success of a course and the possible rewards it may provide in the workplace so levels of motivation can differ greatly. Because of this diversity, it is impossible to identify all of the issues that might arise but they can be categorised according to overriding themes. BACP: U&C, the division of **BACP**, has developed a categorisation system to help with monitoring issues that students bring to sessions and a copy of this can be found accessed through the BACP: U&C.

Mental wellbeing

According to the Mental Health Foundation (**http://www.mentalhealth. org.uk/help-information/mental-health-statistics/**):

- One in four people will experience some kind of mental health problem in the course of a year, although this has recently been disputed (see **http://www.guardian.co.uk/commentisfree/2010/ apr/24/one-in-four-mental-health-statistic**)
- Mixed anxiety and depression is the most common mental disorder in Britain
- Women are more likely to have been treated for a mental health problem than men
- About 10 per cent of children have a mental health problem at any one time
- Depression affects one in five older people
- Suicides rates show that British men are three times more likely to die by suicide than British women
- Self-harm statistics for the UK show one of the highest rates in Europe: 400 per 100,000 of the population
- Only 1 in 10 prisoners has no mental disorder.

Jargon and language

As with working in any specialism, there are terms used that are particular to working in education. In fact this is one of the worst areas to work in if you dislike acronyms which seem to proliferate throughout the whole sector! To help with this, throughout the book you will find all acronyms will be in **bold** lettering. At the end of the book there is a List of Abbreviations where all acronyms are explained. Clearly it is not possible to include all terminology you might come across as many organisations develop their own systems but I have included the main acronyms.

Further reading

Bell, E. (1996) *Counselling in Further and Higher Education*. Buckingham: Open University Press.

A detailed text that considers the advancement of counselling in these two core educational settings and a wide range of issues that can arise.

Noonan, E. (1983) *Counselling Young People*. Routledge, 1983.

An excellent little book that covers development, theories, process and relationships when counselling adolescents.

Lees, J. & Vaspe, A. (eds) *Clinical Counselling in Further and Higher Education*. Routledge, 1999.

A collection of ten chapters that explore different aspects of counselling in colleges and universities from context and techniques to establishing groups.

Beynon, A. & Wright, J. (1997) 'Counselling in Educational Settings: Past Experience, Current Practice and Future Implications'. *Pastoral Care in Education: An International Journal of Personal, Social and Emotional Development*, vol. 15:1, 10–14.

Lawton, B., Bradley, A., Collins, J., Holt, C. & Kelly, F. (2010) *BACP: U&C Guidelines for University and College Counselling Services* (2nd edn). Lutterworth: BACP.

Royal College of Psychiatrists (2011) *College Report CR166: Mental Health of Students in Higher Education*. London: RCPsych.

Tatar M. (2001) 'Counsellors perceptions of adolescence'. *British Journal of Guidance & Counselling*, vol. 29, no. 2, 213–231.

The Scottish Government (2012) *Mental Health Strategy for Scotland: 2012–2015*. Edinburgh: Scottish Government.

The Scottish Government (2002) *Choose Life: A National Strategy and Action Plan to Prevent Suicide in Scotland*. Edinburgh: Scottish Government.

Yaqoob, T. (2010) *Sharing Practice in Mental Health Improvement*. Edinburgh: NUS Scotland.

References

Gallacher, J., Crossan, B., Leahy, J., Merrill, B. & Field, J. (2000) *Education for All? Further Education, Social Inclusion and Widening Access.* Available at **http://www.crll.org.uk/knowledge-exchange/ publications/researchreports/** (accessed 16 October 2012).

Gallacher, J., Crossan, B., Field J. & Merrill, B. (2002) 'Learning careers and the social space: exploring the fragile identities of adult returners in the new further education'. *International Journal of Lifelong Education,* vol. 21, no. 6, pp. 493–509.

Chapter 2
Settings

Chapter 1 introduced four main areas where counselling takes place to support students during their course; in this chapter we will examine these more closely. This chapter is not so much for readers who are already established counsellors employed within one of these settings but more for trainees or counsellors currently considering working in a university or college counselling service. If we are counselling in an educational setting, it is useful to understand the nuances of the particular environments and any influence these might have on the way we work.

As with any counselling service, working in education comes with its own culture which this chapter will start to explain. Colleagues and clients will expect us to have a basic understanding of the environment in which we intend to work and although we may well have experience of being a student, this differs greatly from being employed in the sector. We will start with clarifying the differences between settings and highlight any issues particular to working as a counsellor in these surroundings.

The difference between FE and HE

When we first think of Further Education (**FE**) or Higher Education (**HE**), we might immediately assume that FE refers to a college and HE refers to a university. However, although they are often used in this way, the terms Further Education and Higher Education actually refer to the level of course being delivered rather than the institution in which it is being delivered. This means that students enrolled on an Higher National Certificate (**HNC**) course in a college are actually studying an HE course whereas students in the year below at the same institution who are studying a National Qualification (**NQ**) course are enrolled on an FE course. Another key difference other than level is that FE has a different funding structure to HE, making it more straightforward for FE to be mainly delivered within colleges. To sum up, the core differences are:

- Level of course – HE and FE courses are both delivered in colleges and universities
- Funding structure – not just for students (bursaries, grants, etc.) and courses (funding councils) but also for the establishment itself. Much university funding is gained from research activity and the reputation that research attracts whereas research tends to be under-represented in colleges
- Size of campus and student population – although a generalisation, universities tend to be larger than colleges.

Universities

According to Universities UK:

'Institutions have to meet certain criteria to be awarded the title "university". These are assessed by the Quality Assurance Agency on behalf of the Privy Council. The Privy Council is responsible, under the Further and Higher Education Act 1992, for approving the use of the word "university" (including "university college") in the title of a higher education institution.'

The Universities UK website (http://www.universitiesuk.ac.uk/ UKHESector/Pages/OverviewSector.aspx#Q4)

Universities offer courses such as ordinary and honours degrees, HE certificates and diplomas, postgraduate certificates and diplomas and masters' and doctoral programmes.

As of August 2011 there were 115 universities and 165 HE institutions in the UK (**www.universitiesuk.ac.uk**). We have seen a significant increase in the numbers of students attending university over the past few years and within that, a greater level of social and cultural diversity. There are increased numbers of international students enrolling and unfortunately, this rapid growth means that research findings can go out of date very quickly in this constantly changing area. However, almost all universities provide a student counselling facility, although it must be stated that the level of provision can vary greatly between institutions. The major-ity of universities employ paid counsellors but also offer placements for students nearing completion of their course (sometimes referred to as associate counsellors). Here, trainees have the opportunity to work with clients to gain the face-to-face counselling hours they require to pass their course. University counselling services often consist of a team of professionals working together to provide a range of support including counsellors, mental health advisors, doctors and psychiatrists. Most university counselling services advertise their facilities on a dedicated website, often with video clips and availability. This is an excellent way to communicate with the student base as the pages will be linked to the university website and allow access to them in private.

A recent paper published by The Royal College of Psychiatrists included the following under the title *Student Counselling*:

'Nearly all higher education institutions offer counselling services to students. A recent survey indicated that across the UK approximately 4% of university students are seen by counsellors each year for a wide range of emotional and psychological difficulties. Counsellors working in higher education offer their professional skills and can also utilise their understanding of the connections between psychological and academic difficulties, their knowledge of the educational context and their integration with the wider institution. No counselling service would undertake the diagnosis or treatment of severe mental illness but all would consider it important to be sufficiently well informed to recognise the various forms of mental illness and to know when referral to medical and psychiatric services is necessary. The establishment of links to these services for consultation and referral has always been seen as an essential part of the work of a counselling service in a higher education institution.'

Royal College of Psychiatrists (2011:8–9)

Universities often combine a counselling service for students with the opportunity for staff to access counselling services too. There are advantages and disadvantages to this model but it is common for there to be separate counselling teams; one for working with students and the other for working with staff. This reduces any chance of ethical boundaries slipping. Imagine, for example, you are a counsellor employed in a university. Your first client of the day comes in and talks about feeling bullied by their lecturer. Your next client comes in and they are that very same lecturer. How could you remain unaffected by the content of the first session? Knowing that you will not be placed in that situation can be a relief!

Colleges

Historically, colleges focused more on vocational and FE courses than on an academic curriculum although that has changed over time. Colleges deliver GCSEs, A Levels, AS Levels, Highers (in Scotland) and the English Baccalaureate in addition to Ordinary National Certificates (ONCs), Higher National Certificates (HNCs), Higher National Diplomas (HNDs) and foundation degrees. Because of this, the student population was often from traditionally non-academic backgrounds, seconded by employers or school leavers.

There are currently more colleges than universities in the UK. According to EduBase, there are 371 colleges in England and Wales, 37 in Scotland and 6 (down from 16) in Northern Ireland following their merger programme in 2007. At the time of writing, Scotland is currently undergoing a similar merger programme with the country being regionalised to reduce the number of colleges to around 23.

As with universities, there is no single model of counselling provision in colleges. According to the **BACP: U&C** research in 2006–7, many colleges don't provide a counselling service at all. Because of the community nature of colleges, it is less likely that students will have left home to attend their course. Many remain at home or have been living independently before applying for their course. However, there are still distinct issues that can crop up such as:

- Hard-to-reach students who maintain a sporadic course attendance due to a range of different personal issues and often reflect this by missing counselling sessions
- Low confidence when it comes to studying, often due to a negative school experience
- Coping with assessments. This is an area that has become apparent in our counselling service when analysing the statistics of the previous three years. There is a significant peak in requests for counselling sessions and also an increase in attendance within the November, March and June, which just happen to coincide with end of term assessment dates.
- Course-related issues (such as body image issues for dance students).

Outreach centres/community campuses

Community learning centres (**CLC**s) are campuses that are situated some distance from the core institution specifically to engage hard-to-reach students who would otherwise not be able to study. Students attending CLCs that are situated away from central campuses can experience issues that are exacerbated by not feeling like a 'proper student'. In 2007, Gallacher *et al* conducted interviews with students and staff based in FE satellite centres and found:

'our research has indicated that the boundaries between the CLCs and other aspects of the lives of learners can be seen to be more permeable than those found in the main college campuses. The habitus and dispositions of learners reflect their often complex personal lives. Many are single parents, some have histories of illness, many have very limited incomes, and almost all are initially lacking in confidence and very uncertain about their abilities as learners. This reflects their structural positions in terms of class and gender. Rather than feeling the need to leave the complexity of their lives at the door of the CLCs, it is, often explicitly, brought into the learning site.'

Gallacher et al (2007)

Students who attend community learning centres tend to be re-entering education after a long period out of education. Often they endured a negative school experience and as a result, do not connect learning with a positive outcome. They may also juggle fairly chaotic lifestyles that centre around school hours, reducing the available class time to accommodate their family responsibilities. My own experience of teaching in this environment for over sixteen years falls in line with Gallacher *et al*'s findings. Students have been remarkably open and honest about their personal issues but can disappear from class without notice. Class attendance tends to be viewed in a more informal and optional manner with some students adopting a 'drop-in' approach. This makes course statistics such as attendance, retention and success appear unfavourable, so soft indicators, as such, are a better measurement of the true impact of the course. Because of this, these courses are constantly vulnerable to being withdrawn. It may appear that students would be more likely to attend a free counselling service but in fact, they are less likely to. This can be due to location and poor access, or that they may already be attending counselling via their GP or addiction service, or the fact that the course tutor taking a more encouraging and nurturing role that involves additional support and counselling skills to engage with the students.

Open learning

The growth of computer ownership, access to the internet and computer literacy have all increased the popularity of this method of study. Just searching on the internet introduces us to the range of courses that are available to study at home without the need to attend a taught class. The most well-known open learning institution in the UK is the Open University, which began in 1969 and according to its website has 'more than 250,000 students, close to 7,000 tutors, more than 1,200 full-time academic staff and more than 3,500 support and administrative staff' (**http://www8.open.ac.uk/about/main/the-ou-explained/facts-and-figures**).

The majority of students now expect courses to involve an element of IT and, although this might be accepted by students who are comfortable working online, it can be a source of stress for students who do not have access to a computer or the skills required. There are now very few distance learning courses that do not involve some form of online requirement, whether it be to access resources, contact a tutor and other students or to submit evidence of work or assessments. Course materials for open or distance learning courses are provided in a range of formats depending on the subject but include books, handouts, DVDs, CDs, online resources such as a virtual learning environment (**VLE**) and emails.

Figure 2.1 Distance learning

This is a far harder sector to provide counselling for, as students do not attend a campus. Because of this, subject tutors would be recommended to guide students who requested counselling, to their GP. Online counselling is a rapidly growing area but as yet, I have not found a distance learning institution that offers the facility.

Issues particular to counselling in education settings

Here are some widely experienced issues relating to students that can crop up:

- *Being away from home for the first time.* It is common for students, particularly at universities, to have moved out of the family home to study. There are many issues this can raise when combined with the added pressures of studying but feelings of isolation, displacement, fear of independence and homesickness are common.
- *Feelings of isolation.* Attracting a wide and diverse population can result in universities and colleges being a social minefield where transient friendships, bullying and feeling the 'odd one out' are typical.
- *Autonomy.* This might be the first time that the student has had the freedom and independence to be responsible for themselves but unfortunately this does not always mean that the student has the maturity and self-awareness to cope.
- *Poor time management.* This is a very common issue that most students experience at one time or another. Adult education is significantly different from school-based learning, most notably in that deadlines creep up and there is no one to apply pressure on the student to study.
- *Moving from a school to college or university* can require transitional support to compensate for the differences in culture, learning styles and lifestyle, especially if this occurs at the same time as moving out of the family home.
- *The prevalence of holidays.* This cyclic structure with its regular breaks can create fractures within the therapeutic process as students return to the family home or the counselling service is closed over the festive period, Easter, or the long summer holiday.

During term time, students often experience similar issues linked to their progress on their course, which we can come to recognise. Jane, an FE counsellor, has identified some of the main issues that can crop up at set times during the academic term:

Voices

Jane

'I have found the cyclical nature of the academic year to have a huge impact on the themes that clients bring, often crises around endings emerge in the seemingly endless mini-breaks of the academic year; half-terms and holidays mean that we have breaks every six weeks. At the beginning of the year there tends to be issues around fitting in and forming friendships groups. This can be particularly anxiety-provoking for students who have been bullied in the past. The dip in morale that follows Christmas and New Year often brings crises of direction ("Is it worth all this work?"), anxiety about exams and assignment deadlines, fear of failure and fear of success – often most pronounced in adult learners who come from families who have never achieved academically: "What would success mean to them and their place in the family? Would it be an act of betrayal to do better than their parents have done?" There are often questions about how much they deserve to succeed . . .'

We can see from Jane's experience that the counselling relationship has the potential to be disjointed due to regular holidays but, despite this, the academic terms can raise issues that are experienced by more than one client. Beginning a new course with new people from a range of different geographical and social backgrounds can be nerve-wracking, especially if this is the first time a student has lived independently as they can miss the security and comfort of their family home. The middle of the academic year falls around or just after the Christmas holidays for many so this can be a time of great uncertainty as it can seem a very long time until the end of the year in the summer. The impact of being tested can be highly traumatic for students who are unsure of their abilities; this is a very different experience to school exams! I have identified that in our service, there is a notable increase in assessment and exam-related anxiety in November, March and May, which are the end of our three annual terms so we try to ensure that we can cope with the increased demand during these months.

Summary

- Further Education and Higher Education (FE and HE) refer to a different level of course rather than an educational establishment.
- Universities are considered to be academic and colleges to be vocational, although this distinction is becoming more blurred.
- Universities are often but not always larger than colleges.
- Regular holidays can impact on the therapeutic relationship.
- Students who attend community learning centres are less likely to engage in counselling offered by the course provider.
- Open/Distance learning institutions find it hard to offer this type of personal support.

Further reading

Books and articles

Balestra, E. (2012) 'Challenges in Working with Hard-to-Reach Students in Further Education'. *AUCC Journal*, May 2012, 19–21.

Cahill, J. (2008) 'Counselling in Higher and Further Education'. *R8 Information Sheet*. Lutterworth: BACP.

Chester, A. & Glass, C. (2006) 'Online Counselling: A Descriptive Analysis of Therapy Services on the Internet'. *British Journal of Guidance & Counselling*, vol. 34, no. 2, 145–160.

Collins, J. (2008) 'The Counsellor, The Client and The Organisation'. *AUCC Journal*, September 2008, 6–7.

Cooper, M., Rowland, N., McArthur, K., Pattison, S., Cromarty, K. & Richards, K. (2010) 'Randomised Controlled Trial of School-based Humanistic Counselling for Emotional Distress in Young People: Feasibility Study and Preliminary Indications of Efficacy'. *Child and Adolescent Psychiatry and Mental Health*, vol. 4, no. 12.

Crawley, A. (2009) *Supporting Online Students: A Practical Guide*. San Fransisco: Jossey-Bass.

Feltham, M. & Howdin, J. (2009) 'Organisations Behaving Badly: From Anxiety to Creativity'. *AUCC Journal*, May 2009, 12–14.

Ford, T., Hamilton, H., Meltzer, H. & Goodman, R. (2008) 'Predictors of Service Use for Mental Health Problems Among British Schoolchildren'. *Child and Adolescent Mental Health*, vol. 13, no. 1, 32–40.

Gallacher, J., Crossan, B., Mayes, T., Cleary, P., Smith, L. & Watson, D. (2007) 'Expanding our understanding of the learning cultures in community-based Further Education'. *Educational Review*, 59:4, 501–517.

Knox, H. (2006) *Scoping Study on Transition Support for Students with Mental Health Difficulties*. Scotland: University of Paisley.

Royal College of Psychiatrists (2011) *College Report CR166: Mental Health of Students in Higher Education*. London: RCPsych.

Tait, A. (2000) 'Planning Student Support for Open and Distance Learning'. *Open Learning: The Journal of Open, Distance and e-Learning*, vol. 15, no. 3, 287–299.

Warwick, I., Maxwell, C., Simon, A., Statham, J. & Aggleton, P. (2006) 'Mental health and emotional well-being of students in further education – a scoping study'. Thomas Coram Research Unit: University of London.

Zelnick, L. (2011) '"Can I Show You Something Online?" or "How the eLife Comes Alive in Therapy". *Journal of Infant, Child, and Adolescent Psychotherapy*, vol. 10, no. 4, 411–414.

Websites

Colleges Northern Ireland:

Educational establishments in England and Wales:

http://www.education.gov.uk/edubase/about.xhtml

Scotland's College Development Network:

http://www.scotlandscolleges.ac.uk

Chapter 3
Theory and skills

This chapter will cover a range of appropriate theories and skills that might be of use when working with students. Rather than provide a detailed overview of each theory, which you might gain from many books on counselling, here we are focusing more on possible challenges from alternative frameworks that we might experience and how the consideration of different schools of thought might help us to understand our client's world. I have concentrated more on the application of the theories to make them relevant to working with our client group.

Figure 3.1 Application of theory

As with all counselling activities, working therapeutically with students has to be firmly grounded on recognised psychological theory. By doing this it ensures that any methods chosen are researched and tested thoroughly with a strong evidence base to support the efficacy of the chosen approach, that there is continuity between the practice of counsellors and that our methodology is possible to replicate which reduces the risk of us doing harm. At the same time, we must maintain a flexibility that allows us to appreciate the individuality and uniqueness of our clients. Each counsellor working within the service will bring their own approaches and structure to their practice along with their own personality and style of working. This chapter will provide an overview of the more typical approaches that are used when working with students as opposed to an in-depth account of counselling theories in general, making it useful for updating information in addition to being a helpful resource at sticky moments and times of difficulty.

Before discussing theory, we need to be clear that we are referring to a testable concept that is based on a prediction (or hypothesis) and backed up with empirical evidence. Theories provide a framework for our understanding in counselling. Not only do they help us understand the client, they also help us to contextualise the client's actions, feelings and decisions. This understanding provides a sound base for developing skills and methods of working with individuals and groups that allow the counsellor to practise in a safe and dynamic manner. As well as many practical approaches that specify ways of being and techniques, there are also some theories that do not have specific skills attached but are more of a philosophical approach which help us to be more aware and appreciative of a client's world.

The theories we will look at here are:

- Humanistic theories
- Behavioural theories
- Cognitive theories
- Psychodynamic theories
- Integrative theory
- Solution-focused theory
- Theories of loss
- Family theories.

Humanistic theories

Despite differing widely in practice, all theories that fall within the humanistic category have several aspects in common. Importantly, they all arise from the assumption that people are basically good. They respect the uniqueness of individuals and value personal experience; all place the client within the centre of the relationship and accept them as being the expert within their own lives. The sessions tend to be non-directive and client-led, meaning that the client has the freedom to focus on what they see as their main issue. Clearly this is likely to develop further but the counsellor is careful not to advise or guide the client.

Person-centred therapy

'Prior to therapy the person is prone to ask himself, often unwittingly, *"What do others think I should do in this situation?"*, *"What would my parents or my culture want me to do?"*, *"What do I think ought to be done?"* . . . During the process of therapy the individual comes to ask himself *"How do I experience this?"*, *"What does it mean to me?"'*

Rogers (1967:103)

Person-centred therapy (**PCT**) was developed by Carl Rogers in the 1940s and was, at the time, a radically new way of working with clients because the focus was on respecting and appreciating the client's world from their own perspective rather than from that of the professional. As a counsellor, we know it is not ethical to work with family or friends so we are never going to work with people who are previously known to us. Therefore the client will be the only person within the relationship who knows the situation, knows any other people involved, knows their thoughts and feelings and knows how they feel about the past, present and future. The PCT approach acknowledges and values this in several ways. The use of core conditions such as empathy, congruence and unconditional positive regard ensure that the client is understood, warmly accepted and the relationship is built on honest and genuine interactions. The concept of the actualising tendency presupposes that the client knows what is best even if they are not currently aware of it. This is pertinent in an educational setting as, when handled carefully, this level of trust and belief can have a considerable impact upon the decisions and choices that the client might make in their role as a student. The idea that providing a supportive environment is the main constituent to empowering a student to develop and grow may well be optimistic but it also demonstrates the belief and trust placed in an individual's ability to recognise and act upon their own needs and wants. This approach is generally felt to be appropriate for almost all clients but if a student is feeling out of control, swamped or lacking in direction this supportive and encouraging approach can be the catalyst required to promote self-reflection and self-discovery in an honest and safe relationship. For some it is the counsellor sitting gently within the client's world and being the first person they know who's not telling them what to do. That is the most powerful aspect.

Transactional analysis

'The philosophical assumptions of transactional analysis can be summed up in three statements: People are OK. Everyone has the capacity to think. People decide their own destiny, and these decisions can be changed.'

Stewart (2007:3)

Eric Berne developed his theory of transactional analysis (**TA**) over many years as a direct result of his experiences and observations working as a psychoanalyst. He found that we all alter the way we communicate often, even during a single dialogue. This led to the gradual establishment of the identification of the different ways in which we communicate and how they can lead to interpersonal complications. He was interested in Alfred Adler's notion of a 'life goal', which Berne extended to become a 'life script'. We all have a sense of what we are able and not able to achieve in life; this is formulated over time from early childhood. Our innate sense of accomplishment is influenced in many ways (including by parents, friends, school) and leads us to self-determine how far we can push ourselves. Within an educational setting, this concept can be critical to the potential success of a student: those with confidence who actually believe they are able to pass their course are more likely to succeed than those who feel they will be 'found out' at any moment. Berne's identification of three different ego states (parent, adult and child) is also relevant when we consider the client's self-image of themselves in the role of student; the process of having to start from scratch with a new subject or unlearn a previous understanding, to update themselves or find themselves classed as unskilled can have a negative impact upon any student. The removal of a sense of proficiency can lead to a feeling of naivety or stupidity which can be reflected within the way we interact with those around us. This can be a downside of learning and a client may find that they become defensive, aggressive, demotivated or disinterested as a result. There is a parallel here with the role of a child; moving forward from a position of ignorance can be slow and fraught with error and the accompanying frustrations, lead to an altered way of conversing which in turn can lead to arguments. Many students, no matter what their age, find that they experience periods where instead of communicating as an adult or parent, they communicate in a more childlike fashion which might not have been realised until entering counselling. Finally, Berne's opinion that the individual is able to take control of their reactions and feelings is very encouraging as it places the power and ability to change firmly within the hands of the client.

Existential theory

'[in] existential counselling clients are not viewed as being sick; rather they are seen as being sick of life or awkward at living . . . such people need help in surveying the terrain and in discovering their own best way.'

Corey (1991: 174)

Although mainly a philosophy as opposed to a counselling approach, existentialism plays its part in education-based counselling. This is mainly due to the notion that our external circumstances might certainly limit our choices but they do not determine them; we are able to exercise choice and take command of our own life. Helping a client to view their life in this more accepting way can be both empowering and enlightening. For example, if a student attending counselling is experiencing anxiety and stress due to assessments and exams, they may well be simply focusing on the negative and pressurised aspects of their life. As counsellors, we might help a client see their current situation within the context of other aspects of their life such as their family, friends, achievements, progress and abilities. This increase in self-awareness can be a potent tool in supporting a client to re-evaluate their current challenges and to re-establish control. The underpinning ideology guides us to identify aspects of choice so we are able to re-establish control and direction. With a client who is experiencing significant amounts of stress, the idea that they are able to regain control over aspects of their life can be very powerful, even the concept of taking responsibility for those choices and any potential outcome can be sufficient for some to make the difference between passing a course or dropping out. This search for meaning, purpose and context in their current situation might establish links between aspects such as study, family, relationships and self to help them articulate how they view themselves and essentially, who they are. The concept of authenticity is a core factor; we have to be honest about who we are and how we live if we are to live authentically. By that I mean we have to acknowledge that if we make our own decisions then we have to accept and live with the consequences whether they be good or bad. An example here would be if a married client began an affair. They might be happy to continue and manage any personal feelings of guilt because it is outweighed by the excitement or pleasure in the secret relationship. However, to be authentic, they must also accept that if their actions are discovered, it was their decision to start an affair and therefore there will be consequences which they have to take responsibility for.

Gestalt theory

'Our view of the therapist is that he is similar to what a chemist calls a catalyst, an ingredient which precipitates a reaction which might not otherwise occur.'

Perls et al (1984:15)

Working from a gestalt model changes the perspective of the session. Instead of spending time concentrating on the past or the future, the here and now takes centre stage. Rather than worry about the future (which we can identify through use of language such as *'What if . . .'* and *'But it might happen'*), the client and counsellor remain in the present and consider how the client's world actually is in this moment. By using this approach, we avoid the negativity of spending time with situations and experiences we can no longer change or fretting un-necessarily about what might or might not yet happen. We would not be ignoring what happened to our client in the past but we would be more concerned as to how it was affecting them now rather than then. We would also be helping the client to consider the current focus they are using; even small challenges can seem enormous if they are taken out of context and loom in the foreground. As this approach can sometimes be challenging, a trusting, honest and safe relationship with the counsellor is of great importance. Here are two examples of how we might recognise a client talking of their past or future. They might bring up:

1. How they missed their Dad when they were growing up where the counsellor could encourage them to consider how they miss their Dad today, or
2. How sure they are that they will fail their exams despite not having sat them yet. Here the counsellor might focus more on the current feeling of failure than the future exams.

Behavioural theories

'A reflex is an involuntary, unlearned, predictable response to a given stimulus (or class of stimuli), a response that is not influenced by any conscious thought or resolution, but that can usually be seen to have some clear purpose in protecting the organism or helping it to adjust to its environment.'

Miller (1966:195)

Classical and operant conditioning

Behavioural psychology is based on the assumption that we are all born as a blank slate and who and how we are today is a direct result of our learning and interaction with our environment. This is good news as behaviourists also argue that anything that we have learned can also be unlearned using the same techniques that we used to learn the behaviour in the first place. Two of these methods of associative learning were identified as *Classical Conditioning* by Ivan Pavlov and *Operant Conditioning* by B.F. Skinner. Classical conditioning might explain a student who panics when they see desks laid out in exam formation in a hall as although the desks themselves cannot cause any harm, the student is making an association between the desks, their layout and personal feelings of exams stress. A similar example of operant conditioning might be a student who has stopped studying despite achieving A grades all year. They have learned that they always gain an A for their work; they assume it will happen so there is no need to study. However, if occasionally they scored a B or C, it might motivate them to continue applying themselves to their work. The issue here is that the reward of an A grade has lost its impact and is being taken for granted. When it comes to working therapeutically with this approach, there are some theorists and practitioners who refer to methods using classical conditioning as *behaviour therapy* and methods using operant conditioning as *behaviour modification*, although this is not universal. An example of a technique based on classical conditioning is *exposure therapy*, where the client is placed in the situation they have been fearful of, for example, sitting in an exam hall. After a sufficient period of time when no harm has come to them it is hoped that the fear will have become extinct. Were they made to take part in a real exam for an extended period of time it would be using *flooding* but if they are asked to imagine the situation whilst sitting in the empty hall it would be *implosion therapy*. If they were gently encouraged into the exam hall stage by stage, we would be using *systematic desensitisation*.

Applying operant conditioning is also possible with this example: the introduction of a *token economy*, whereby the student is rewarded every time they sit an exam might be a motivating tool, whereas punishing them for avoiding exams would fall under the title of aversion therapy. Clearly there are significant ethical implications to consider here!

Social learning theory

Albert Bandura's social learning theory (**SLT**) took both forms of behavioural conditioning into consideration but developed the idea further identifying additional methods of learning. Bandura felt that cognitive processes had to be considered when understanding how and why we do things. He argued that we learn from the experiences of others (vicarious learning) and imitating or modelling ourselves on others who we would like to be like which is known to be particularly prevalent during adolescence. The mindset and expectations of the student will also have an influence of their experiences; if they have been a successful student in the past they will have a greater expectation to succeed now but of course that works the other way round too. If working in FE with a client who had a very negative school experience, they may expect to fail here too. This mental pre-programming can pre-determine an outcome by becoming a self-fulfilling prophecy. There are, according to Bandura, methods of influencing an individual's level of self-efficacy such as introducing them to someone who has been successful in an area the student has self doubts about as a way of boosting their confidence. Alternatively, positive support and encouragement from family, friends, tutors and peers can persuade a student that they are capable of success. Reducing irrational anxiety surrounding a situation is another method of encouraging success. Originally focusing only on observable behaviour and dismissing the influence of thought process and motivation on our actions, therapists now acknowledge the association with cognitive processes and the methodology is more likely to be blended into a more integrated approach known as cognitive behavioural therapy (**CBT**).

Cognitive theories

'Cognitive therapy seeks to ameliorate clients' emotional distress by helping them to identify, examine and modify the distorted and maladaptive thinking underlying their distress.'

Neenan and Dryden (2004:xi)

Leading on from Bandura's social learning theory, cognitive theories focus more on the client's thought processes and less on their behaviour than the behavioural and CBT approaches. It is a perspective that considers our perception, the way we make sense of the world around us, how we do or do not apply logic to our thinking processes and how we are prone to distorting the reality of what happens to us with what we think that means to us. Although Jean Piaget's theory may be helpful if working with children, when working with adults we are more likely to refer to approaches developed by Albert Ellis (**REBT**) and Aaron Beck (**CT**).

Rational emotive behavioural therapy

Albert Ellis's work focused heavily on reducing the damaging distortions that we are very skilful at creating in our minds. Rational emotive behavioural theory (REBT) is founded on the assumption that we all want to be happy but when things happen around us or to us, we respond with feelings and reactions to that event. Sometimes our responses are positive but often we develop a belief about a situation that is irrational and leads to unhappiness. Ellis developed the following ABC format to illustrate the relationship between our beliefs and our reactions:

'A. Something happens. B. You have a belief about the situation. C. You have an emotional reaction to the belief.'

Ross (2006)

If we apply this to a relevant situation, we might consider a student who attends counselling as:

A. Their lecturer has indicated that they are not doing as well as they could and will need to study hard to pass their exams.
B. The client believes that they will fail and be judged as useless.
C. They feel panicked and inadequate.

However, if the client has a different belief, the student will have a different emotional outcome:

A. Their lecturer has indicated that they are not doing as well as they could and will need to study hard to pass their exams.
B. The client believes they will have to increase the time they study if they are to succeed.
C. They feel motivated and structured.

In a counselling session, we can help the client to highlight the application of logic and reason during examination of the belief stage that can in turn, influence their emotional response. Ellis focused on the fixed ideas we develop regarding what we must or should do or what must or should happen for us to be happy. When the client investigates and challenges these assumptions, we can witness them realising that there are other more positive beliefs that result in a healthier emotional outcome.

Cognitive therapy

Aaron Beck developed cognitive therapy (**CT**), which is very similar indeed to Ellis's REBT, although it is less directive and more person-centred in approach. Beck also highlights cognitive distortion and the ability we all have for interpreting our world according to our own beliefs. However, one core difference is that whilst Ellis focuses on our irrational 'shoulds' and 'musts' that can negatively influence our emotional responses, Beck highlights the way we develop unjustified predictions or consequences. A second difference is regarding the role of the counsellor. While Ellis was more of a prescriptive teacher who pointed out distortions to the client, Beck sees a warm therapeutic relationship as essential where the client is encouraged to recognise the distortions themselves.

Multi-modal therapy

Arnold Lazarus developed multi-modal therapy (**MMT**) in the 1970s as a method of working with clients in a more holistic way that provided a unique framework for working in a structured manner with all clients:

'The underlying assumption [. . .] is that because individuals are troubled by a variety of specific problems, it is appropriate that a multitude of treatment strategies be used in bringing about change.'

Corey (1991:308).

He designed the system below to help the counsellor focus on each aspect separately to provide a comprehensive approach:

B   Behavioural
A   Affect (moods, emotions, feelings)
S   Sensation (five senses)
I   (self-image, memories and dreams)
C   Cognition (beliefs, insights, attitudes, opinions, ideas, thinking styles)
I   Interpersonal (how we socially interact)
D   Drugs and biology (physical health, medications, substances, nutrition, exercise, general health, sleep).

These areas are considered to be preliminary prompts helping us un-cover themes that might emerge within the first stage of working with our client. Once these are identified, we might work at the relationship between each category before the final stage which is to identify coping strategies. Often when working with students, it becomes apparent that there are several aspects to their way of being that influence their cogni-tive processes, so this framework can be useful.

Psychodynamic theories

Psychodynamic theories share underpinning assumptions which can be useful to bear in mind when working with clients. Aspects such as the control our unconscious has in determining our choices, behaviours and feelings and that our experiences during our childhood development impact on our personality as an adult can all be enlightening. This is a wide-ranging and complex approach which requires significant training and experience to balance successfully these assumptions if we are to integrate them into the therapeutic relationship that we find is preferred when counselling students.

Psychoanalytical theory

'It is only on a dissection of hysterical mental processes that the manifold nature of the problems of consciousness becomes apparent.'

Freud (1900:324)

Sigmund Freud's psychoanalytical approach brings in a range of techniques to focus on balance of the ego states and the unconscious such as dream analysis and free association to analyse the psyche. Traditionally a complex, long-term and highly involved therapy, it is more likely that psychoanalytical counsellors working in educational settings are working on the assumption that bringing the unknown into the realm of the known is in itself a healing process (self-awareness → insight → positive change).

When working in education, a reoccurring theme is defence mechanisms, which, according to Freud, are methods we employ to prevent us from feeling the hard truth of a situation, a way to protect ourselves. This can be a common experience when working with students who are experiencing extended periods of stress, particularly if they are adolescents (Geldard & Geldard, 2010:11). There are many defence mechanisms identified, some of which are more apparent than others in this client group, such as *compensation*, where we replace what we consider to be our weaknesses with behaviours we think are more acceptable. An example could be a student bullying others when they are afraid of being bullied themselves, or *denial*, where we refuse to accept that an event ever took place, for example when a student continues with two part-time jobs to support themselves financially while simultaneously failing the course due to no time to study. *Rationalisation* is used on a regular basis by young people as they try to explain unacceptable behaviours in a way that makes more sense to them such as not doing homework because their friend has promised them a copy of theirs, so it is a waste of time to both be doing the same work. Another common defence mechanism is *reaction formation*, which emerges when we are uncomfortable with our true feelings so might behave in the opposite way and so prevent others realising it. This is one of the reasons that young people hit each other in a playful way when they are attracted to each other. There are others such as repression, sublimation and dissociation.

Adlerian theory

Adler's theory of individual psychology differed from Freud's psychoanalytical approach in that it considers our social connectedness rather than viewing us in isolation. According to Adler, our relationships with others have a great impact on our mental wellbeing as does the uniqueness of our upbringing. In fact, the way we interpret our experience is more important to our mental health than what actually took place. It is clear to see how this can be relevant to clients who are part of a student community and the social interactions that can be associated with that. Adler believed that our place within our family (birth order) and the influence of our parents have the greatest impact upon the way we learn to interact with others. Adler was very interested in perceived feelings of inferiority and the impact that this can have on us, of the power of our conscious mind, but disagreed with Freud's focus on sexual urges. When a student finds themselves as part of a learning population, the expectations can be overwhelming with many students doubting their abilities on several fronts: socially, academically, emotionally or culturally. Individual psychology highlights the necessity to be successful in social relationships as well as not feeling inferior to others academically for students to remain happy and healthy during their time studying.

Attachment theory

Like Adler, John Bowlby and later, Mary Ainsworth were most interested in familial relationships and our bonding with our carers as a child. Bowlby argued that the strength of the bond we develop with our caregiver as a baby impacts on the way we interact socially as an adult, our level of pro-social or anti-social behaviour and how secure we feel. According to Bowlby, in our early childhood we learn whether we are able to trust others or not which in turn impacts on how we form lifespan attachments with people we consider to be irreplaceable.

- Children who developed a secure attachment will develop into confident adults who are able to make balanced choices and are comfortable in a loving relationship.
- Insecure or avoidant attachment results from a lack of emotional input from the parent resulting in an emotionally withdrawn child. As adults they will find it harder to form emotional connections with others, preferring self-reliance.
- An unreliable, unpredictable relationship can lead to a resistant or ambivalent bond. The inconsistency in the parent's response can lead to the child trying to work out which of their behaviours receives the most desirable response. As an adult, they may distrust the affection of their partner, in turn making them unpredictable themselves.
- Disorganised attachment results from a relationship where a parent or parents constantly change rules and criticise the child for not adhering to the rules. This lack of clarity, structure and security leads to an adult who is conflicted between wanting love but not trusting the relationship.

Bowlby felt that if a child does not receive a secure loving relationship with its mother during the first two years of its life, it can result in lower intelligence, criminality, depression, increased aggression and an inability to demonstrate emotion as an adult.

Voices

John

'Since attending a continuing professional development (CPD) workshop on attachment theory several years ago, I have found that it has become one of the main frameworks that I view my clients through. So many students seem to experience attachment issues, not simply obvious ones like having left home for the first time, but quite significant relationship issues with their parents. I have lost count of the number of time clients realise that much of their upset has been caused by a parent who has treated them in a way that has been harmful.'

Integrative theory

This is arguably the most common counselling approach used at present. The belief that more than one theoretical model can be integrated to provide a more specific and individual therapy for our clients has been increasing since the 1970s. We have already covered some integrated therapies such as **REBT** (cognitive and behavioural) and **TA** (humanistic and psychodynamic). There is much discussion regarding the methodology of combining theories but with 'integration' (as opposed to 'eclecticism'), a counsellor might choose to combine two or more theories that share the same basic assumptions about the human psyche. Gerard Egan used this approach when he developed his 'Skilled Helper' model where Stage 1 is grounded in humanistic psychology, Stage 2 is grounded in humanistic and cognitive psychology and Stage 3 is grounded in humanistic and behavioural psychology. This structure allows the counsellor the freedom and flexibility to shape a focused and individual approach for the client whilst remaining within a sound theoretical base. This approach is popular and appropriate when working within any educational setting as it allows the counsellor to adapt and respond to the client depending upon their maturity, situation, feelings, reactions and readiness to engage with a therapeutic approach. This flexibility is well-suited to the unexpected and unpredictable nature of counselling students.

Solution-focused theory

This is a very different approach that has been shown to work well in educational settings (White, 2003) because the locus of attention is the positive coping mechanisms of the client (solution-talk) rather than the negativity of areas that are troublesome (problem-talk). Rather than spending time concentrating on challenges, barriers or problems, the counsellor redirects the client to identify their strengths, how they have successfully overcome issues in the past and how they would recognise when positive change occurred. The 'miracle question' is used regularly to help re-ground the sessions which can be worded differently depending on the client but centres around the query 'If this problem disappeared, how would you know it?'. This allows the client to concentrate on positive aspects without involving negative thinking. Drawing attention away from the difficulty and towards ways of managing alters the tone of the relationship, allowing the client to leave with a sense of achievement and strength. Five very simple guidelines are provided by O'Connell (2003), which are:

- If it isn't broken, don't fix it.
- Small change can lead to bigger changes.
- If it's working, keep doing it.
- If it's not working, stop doing it.
- Keep therapy as simple as possible.

Theories of loss

Loss appears time and time again when counselling in adult education as it affects each and every one of us so many times throughout our lives. Here we are not simply referring to death and bereavement, although that is of course also relevant. Loss can creep up in the form of relationships ending, loss of a partner, arguments, the loss of friendships, failing an exam, loss of self-belief, losing a job, loss of money or status or even a tooth, or loss of appearance. There are many theories to help us understand the process of loss which tend to refer to stages (Kubler-Ross), features (Murray-Parkes) or tasks (Warden) during the process but it is important to remember not to try to 'insert' a client into a particular stage or point in a theory. The theories are there to help us understand, not to label or pigeonhole clients. Loss is an issue that transcends age, culture, gender and ability making it one of the most recurring we might come across. If you would like to understand more about the subject of loss from a counselling perspective, there is a title in this series called *Challenges in Counselling: Loss* by Sally Flatteau-Taylor.

Family theories

These are theories that are less likely to be used within our sector because they are most often used in the context of family therapy. For some, there is even a requirement to become a temporary honorary family member but despite this, they can be very useful for providing a framework which we can use to help understand our client's world. On the one hand we know that families can contribute greatly to unhappiness, through instability, changing relationships, neglect or control and power issues but conversely, many other students claim their family can be the greatest source of help and support during difficult times (Fox *et al*, 2001). These theories all share the common theme that they reduce the focus or blame from the individual and place it clearly on the family unit and the general interpersonal relationships and connections.

Family systems theory

Family systems theory views the family as a collection of relationships that involve specific behaviours and patterns. Any systems theory works by deconstructing and reconstructing the area under consideration which in family systems theory are the interpersonal systems that evolve and develop over time within family groups. These are informal, invisible and tend to be based on unspoken rules. Within the reconstruction stage during therapy, the concept of cohesion or interconnection and solidity is emphasised with the intention of encouraging families to come together. Any individual problems experienced by family members (and the resulting family interactions) can perpetuate difficulties and are apparent even between generations, particularly if assortive mating has taken place. Minuchin (1974) identified an absence of clear rules as potentially leading to no workable authority structure as there is not the security to be found in predictable stability. This lack of a power hierarchy can lead to mixed subsystems and cliques. As counsellors we might consider the unspoken boundaries or lack of boundaries as a potential source of confusion for our client. Our clients therefore are the product of their environment and can find it difficult to adjust to the structure within educational settings.

Family dysfunction model

Similarly, the family dysfunction model takes the view of the family being a constantly developing entity that is never static. Within this domestic unit there can be collusion between different members, so the children can be just as active in the normalisation of dysfunctional behaviours as the adults can such as in perpetuating dysfunctional behaviours such as multidirectional aggression (when parents and children are aggressive towards each other). A shift in the value base takes place and harmful behaviours are normalised which can also lead to changing of expected roles within the household. This can often result from parents over- or under-compensating for behaviours they experienced whilst growing up. We can see that this might have a similar impact on students to the previous theory where there is a difficulty with roles, structure and boundaries.

Family adjustment model

Within this model, historical factors are important so the previous experiences of our client shapes how they learn to deal with things in the present. They will have learned particular coping resources and strategies within their family instead of successfully managing challenges. The strength of their family social support determines their perceived isolation but all three aspects are interlinked in a reciprocal relationship. Members of the family may experience a shift in the traditional roles within the family unit. An example of this might be an adolescent who has grown up in the role of parent, caring for their younger siblings when their parent or parents were absent. We might find them presenting as being resentful of their enforced role but equally, they might associate with the role's adult responsibilities and be resentful of guidance or control.

Family interaction model

This theory concentrates on one or more issues within a family such as addiction, illness or disability. Essentially, each family member plays out a role to maintain the status quo, providing a comfort zone. Difficulties might occur when the issue is alleviated or reduced. This game-playing can be cyclical and self-reinforcing and as before, can be evident between generations. The family interaction model is often used when working with a client living with an addiction. Each member has to take responsibility for the part they play in facilitating the behaviours surrounding the original issue.

Additional modalities

We have only touched the surface of the vast range of approaches we might find in counselling services in educational institutions. Another range which we have not touched on here is the use of creative approaches which can be appreciated by students who fear the intensity of a one-to-one session. Initially, using 'props' can appear to provide a distraction, but alternatively, as FE counsellor Jane found, therapies that do not focus on spoken language are useful when working with a range of clients:

Voices

Jane

'I did a Diploma in Person-Centred Art Therapy Skills. The intention behind this was to support working with clients for whom English is not their first language and communication can be difficult, and for working with clients with learning disabilities. I now use this method frequently with a wide range of clients.'

Further reading

Colledge, R. (2002) *Mastering Counselling Theory*. Palgrave MacMillan, 2002.

An easy-to-read and pertinent book that covers eighteen popular counselling theories.

Flatteau-Taylor, S. (2013) *Challenges in Counselling: Loss*. London: Hodder Education.

A book in this series for those who would like to understand more about the subject of loss from a counselling perspective.

Joseph, S. (2001) *Theories of Counselling and Psychotherapy: An Introduction to the Different Approaches*. Palgrave MacMillan, 2001.

A text aimed at trainees that explains counselling theory in the context of practice including case studies.

Nelson-Jones, R. (2010)*Theory and Practice of Counselling and Therapy* (5th edn). London: Sage.

This book covers counselling theories in more detail but remains straightforward and relevant.

References

Corey, G. (1991) *Theory and Practice of Counseling and Psychotherapy* (4th edn). California: Brooks/Cole.

Fox, P., Caraher, M. & Baker, H. (2001) 'Promoting Student Mental Health'. *The Mental Health Foundation*, vol. 2, no. 11.

Freud, S. (1900) *The Interpretation of Dreams.*

Geldard , K. & Geldard, D. (2010) *Counselling Adolescents: The Proactive Approach for Young People*. London: Sage.

Miller, G.A. (1966) *Psychology: The Science of Mental Life*. Reading: Penguin.

Minuchin, S. (1974) *Families and Family Therapy*. London: Tavistock.

O'Connell, B. (2003) 'Introduction to the Solution-Focused Approach'. In *Handbook of Solution-Focused Therapy*. London: Sage.

Perls, F., Hefferline, R.F. & Goodman, P. (1984) *Gestalt Therapy: Excitement and Growth in the Human Personality*. London: Souvenir Press.

Rogers, C. (1967) *On Becoming a Person*. London: Constable & Robinson.

Ross, W. (2006) *What is REBT?* Available at **http://www.rebtnetwork. org/whatis.html** (accessed 3 January 2013).

Stewart, I. (2007) *Transactional Analysis Counselling in Action* (3rd edn). London: Sage.

White, N. (2003) 'The Solution-Focused Approach in Higher Education'. In *Handbook of Solution-Focused Therapy*, O'Connell, B. and Palmer, S. (eds) (London: Sage).

Chapter 4
Identifying anxieties

The *raison d'être* of this book is to identify and help work with common worries and concerns that are specific to working with our client group. I have focused on the ten main issues that were raised recently by members of the **BACP: U&C** in response to an email requesting them to identify any difficulties they encountered regularly. Clearly, it is not possible to cover all areas of concern here and I should emphasise that I have not placed these in any particular order. Once we have identified the anxieties here, we will be considering possible strategies for working with these issues in the following chapter.

1. Financial constraints on counselling services

We are seeing major restructuring within the education sector; an ongoing process as funding is reduced or reallocated and departments are expected to account for their expenditure and budget management. This will and has resulted in counselling services having to look inwards at their costings and the services that they are able to offer. Primary costs involve the number of paid counsellors a service employs and whether they are full- or part-time. Many services are supplementing their provision with offering trainee placements and opportunities for volunteer counsellors working towards their accreditation. Although these are reasonable and indeed necessary within a profession (imagine if medical students, teachers or indeed hairdressers had no opportunity to practise before qualifying), they do raise discussions surrounding the safety, support, mentoring and competency of a service.

In addition to staffing, there are environmental costs such as premises, furniture, computers and stationery, marketing and publicity costs and professional costs such as supervision and continuing professional development (**CPD**). Core funding might be provided by an institution's internal budgeting but it is becoming more common that funding is being sought from external sources, for example; from Additional Learning Support (**ALS**) budgets. This ties in with the dilemmas surrounding the passing on of information discussed in *4. Relationship between counselling and academic outcomes* below. Generally, when it comes to funding, the manager of the counselling service is bombarded from several different directions.

2. Working with hard-to-reach students

Who are we referring to here? Who are 'hard-to-reach students'? Possibly due to the vocational associations within Further Education (**FE**), traditionally colleges are often assumed to attract students with a less focused approach to education and studying than universities. However, with widening participation agendas, social inclusion policies and articulation agreements, universities are also recognising that their student population may not be drawn solely from the traditional social and academic circles that they once were. Students from non-academic backgrounds may have different aspirations, learning styles and support mechanisms than students from more expected backgrounds. The upbringing, socialisation and home life of a student on their own by no means defines our 'hard-to-reach' population. There are many reasons or barriers for students who may well benefit from counselling to present as a did not attend (**DNA**):

- Students may view attending counselling as admitting they are not able to cope
- Their ongoing issues may prevent them from attending regularly
- They may not be able to afford any additional travel/childcare costs to attend
- Any chaos in their lives may overtake the need to attend the session
- Work commitments can reduce time available to attend
- A counselling session can become yet another appointment to add to mounting pressures
- Peer pressure may prevent them from engaging with support
- A mental illness may make it difficult to cope with attending regular sessions
- They may simply forget.

Figure 4.1 Working with hard-to-reach students

For me, the core of the issue lies with whether we accept **DNA**s as an indicator of an underlying issue or rather whether we view them as a sign of failure. What we as counsellors need to do, is reflect on our practice to ensure that we are meeting the needs of our increasingly diverse student populations.

3. Counselling staff and students

Many counselling departments offer counselling for both students and staff. This can raise several difficulties in our practice, for example:

- Environment – students and staff sharing a space in a combined service. Both client groups may feel distinctly uncomfortable with the possibility of meeting someone they know when they attend their counselling sessions.
- Counsellors – potential overlapping of boundaries if working with both client groups. A situation may occur whereby a student client discusses a member of staff they are experiencing difficulties with which compromises the counsellor who may also be working with that same individual, or vice versa.
- Funding – different funding streams. Separating financial sources for students and staff can cause complications. An example of this would be providing two separate sets of end of year statistics.

- Management – split responsibilities of outcomes between academic (students) and occupational health (staff). Managing two parallel teams of counsellors who may be working in two separate environments is not easy. Employing one manager for each service can be costly and be perceived as duplication.

This is by no means a comprehensive list but highlights some of the core questions that must be asked prior to setting up or evaluating a counselling service that caters for both students and staff.

4. Relationship between counselling and academic outcomes

Which is our greatest aim; students' emotional or psychological wellbeing, or our clients' retention and success on their course? Do we measure our success with a therapeutic outcome measure such as **CORE-OM**, or do we measure the outcome using course attendance and results? The difficulty with this question is that whilst the counselling service might answer without hesitation that the students' wellbeing is central to our practice, university and college managers may be far more focused on the latter. This can lead to tensions in the relationship between the service and management of an academic institution.

In addition to this is the challenge of the collation and dissemination of the data itself. We have strict requirements surrounding confidentiality and yet a growing number of services are being requested to provide information regarding their clients to satisfy funding bodies or to justify their existence in the eyes of management. Here we can find ourselves stuck in the situation of being asked for information that compromises our professional or ethical position whilst being instructed that if we do not provide it, then it could be perceived that we are creating barriers, not working transparently or preventing a student from accessing financial support. This can be incredibly stressful, especially for lone workers or when the request is worded in such a way that it appears to be mandatory.

5. Threat of outsourcing

The reoccurring theme of saving money by providing services more cheaply is ongoing. As counsellors we constantly have to justify expenditure, which can be disheartening and exhausting. The prevalence and cost of an Employee Assistance Programme (**EAP**) is attractive for budget holders who may wish to keep a tight reign over staff support services and occupational health. The possibility that a service may be disbanded and provision relocated to an external agency can be a very real threat to some services. Counsellors can find themselves in a situation where they have to justify their practice, provide evidence for their outcomes and reduce their costs above and beyond the usual professionalism of a service. This is an area that resonates with Jane, the FE counsellor, when she considers the impact that such a situation and the insensitivities of the organisation may have on counselling practice:

Voices

Jane

'Containment – the issue of who contains the container? When a lone worker is holding the distress of an organisation, what support [do] they receive? How little do organisations understand, for example, safeguarding emergencies in a wider context of cuts? When we are not certain of our own security in our jobs, how can we offer a secure base to frightened clients?'

We can see from this reflection that the impact of such a process can be far-reaching and the mindset of the staff undergoing this process is key to the atmosphere within the service during this time. The fear of change, of stepping out of our comfort zone, can be accompanied by a sense of lack of control and disempowerment; issues that we work with on a daily basis with clients.

6. Cultural issues

There has been a significant increase in international students enrolling on courses within the UK. This is due to a variety of reasons but two main ones are (1) the reputation and value that British qualifications have gained abroad, attracting an increase in international students, and (2) individuals seeking asylum in the UK but not being allowed to work for the duration of the process. Both of these groups can present with issues as a result of their particular situation; the pressure of succeeding when their families have invested so much in their future, or the incredible stresses that surround personal loss when seeking asylum. These are just two examples of how our client group is changing and why we may see an increase in clients from different cultures seeking counselling.

Understanding of the counselling process differs from culture to culture. Many societies do not have a tradition of counselling; talking about diffi-culties is seen as selfish or a weakness. In many cultures, such matters are more appropriate for discussion with a spiritual leader. If an individual is struggling with an aspect of their life, it can be a source of shame for the family. Many cultures see 'problems' as being shared within a community rather than the personal matter we might see it in our culture.

So we can see that our clients might be approaching counselling with a different expectation, maybe expecting advice or guidance as they would receive from a religious guide, possibly feeling shameful or uncertain about attending in addition to their underpinning issues. We need to ensure that we have prepared ourselves appropriately using supervision, **CPD**, an awareness of other cultures and self-reflection to avoid doing harm.

7. New developments

Up to now we have considered many areas of cutbacks in counselling services. We have acknowledged the financial pressures that managers are facing so here we will focus on how this can impact on our counselling and measures that we might be asked to implement to reduce costs. It is well recognised that one-to-one counselling is the most costly approach to providing support but this is the method we have been trained in, so sits within our comfort zone. Being asked to develop new methods of therapeutic working with clients can be very challenging indeed. Firstly, we must dispel the idea that this might be as a result of us not doing a good job of individual counselling; in education settings, this is unlikely to be the driver behind the suggestion of new approaches. Additional methodologies are about expanding our provision, supporting more students without increasing our costs. The introduction of online counselling, telephone sessions or group work is currently on the agenda of many counselling services. Of course, as with any new innovations such developments come with their own challenges, in this case technologically, legally and ethically. We may hold a fear that our interventions will in some way be diluted, that this is not how we were trained to work or that we don't feel confident enough with alternative methods to trust the therapeutic benefit to our clients. We may also need to be convinced of the efficacy and require evidence of the advantages to new ways of working to warrant the investment of time involved to change.

8. Risk of harm

When we talk of risk of harm, what do we mean by harm, and harm to whom? Rather than only focusing on the client, we should not forget ourselves and our capacity to put our clients' needs before our own. Many anxieties we may have around harm may be in relation to our client, but we are working in an environment where we can also cause harm to ourselves.

Firstly, in relation to our client we may harbour concerns regarding issues such as suicide, risky behaviours, self-harm, neglect, addiction and stress. These are all valid fears and we would not be reflective, professional counsellors if we were not aware of the dangers surrounding these con-cerns. Indeed, as Reeves points out:

'The counsellor in an education setting might be seen as having the specialist knowledge and skills to respond to a client who is self-harming. Often counsellors have more experience than other professionals found in such settings, such as teachers, lecturers or other academic support staff, and will be turned to in response to a crisis (it is not untypical for the disclosure of self-harm to be viewed as a crisis by the person who has been disclosed to).'

Reeves (2013)

This expectation places additional responsibility on the counsellor. The weight of this presumption is stressful enough. How we engage with a client who has trusted us enough to share their situation with us can be the difference between life and death. Recognising that harm can be unintentional as well as intentional is a good start to formulating a way of working with suffering, hurt and pain.

Interestingly, when we look inwardly at our own risk from harm we may touch on issues such as 'burn-out', self-harm through over-work, stress, working on the very edge of our abilities and fears surrounding isolated working. On the surface these may appear to be unintentional side-effects of working as a counsellor but they are no less dangerous than the potential situations involving harm a client can present with. We are just more likely to accept them as part and parcel of the job. Our reaction to our own situation may be very different to how we might respond if a client divulged similar situations and feelings.

In both cases, with regard to clients and to ourselves, we need to develop a very clear strategy for working with risk of harm.

9. Time constraints and waiting lists

The increasing pressure that counselling services find themselves under is an ongoing and almost universal challenge. Here we can hear the experiences of three counsellors and the effect that juggling restricted availability, **DNA**s and the impact that holidays can have on counselling relationships. First, Heidi, a postgraduate diploma student placement:

Voices

Heidi

'I have offered voluntary counselling at two different colleges and there has always been a high level of last-minute cancellations and DNAs. It was therefore a challenge for me to get the prescribed hours required for my counselling diploma and I needed to take on an extra placement. I often drove a long way to be in the colleges, yet sometimes this was a wasted journey. Also some students were being sent by their tutors and had no real desire to be entering into counselling. I believe they contributed towards the high levels of DNAs. Another challenge at one of the colleges I worked at was in regard to a very vulnerable client who, because of his mental health problems, was asked to leave his course. Our relationship was thus severed without warning, leaving me with grave concerns as to the welfare of my client, he was no longer registered on the course and therefore his counselling could not continue. This occurred during a very crucial stage of counselling.'

We can see here that Heidi felt the pressure of making the effort to attend counselling sessions that clients did not always appreciate, the challenge of trying to engage with clients who did not want to be there at all and finally, of how the status of a student can determine their level of support. If a student leaves, their support ends. She had to achieve a set number of counselling hours to pass her course which placed her under pressure from the start. She experienced sessions being 'wasted' on clients who were referred against their wishes and the opposite, where counselling was withdrawn for a client who was very much in need.

Elaine, a volunteer counsellor working towards her accreditation, identified far more with the challenge of having a restricted number of sessions determined by the organisation and the effect this can have on working with an anxious client:

Voices

Elaine

'With a great proportion of students being mature with ages ranging from 18 to 50 years old, a mature student returns to the education system with fixed conditions of worth. They are often propelled back in time to childhood, anxiety and peer pressure with little or no self-confidence. This is where counselling comes into its own, providing a safe place to discuss these issues and anxieties, and actually have a full-scale battle with anxiety; anxiety thrives in a college student and it loves to see them fail. On the other hand I, as a counsellor, love to get in amongst it with a client, to challenge their anxieties, to encourage self-awareness and growth in their abilities. To enable them to see themselves, their true selves, the individual that has a longing to learn and grow. I can stay with my client's process supporting them while their confidence grows. Although at college we only have a six-week initial contract with the client, we are lucky enough to have a robust enough supply of counsellors to extend this contract, at the counsellors' own discretion. I have made use of this many times especially in cases of anxiety and depression, where the client needs continued support often to the end of the course.'

However, Jane, a counsellor working within a FE college, identified a different source of challenge; she has experienced 'so many breaks to working – every six weeks there's a vacation (abandonment)', which is a situation common to the majority of education providers.

To summarise, the experiences of just three counsellors has identified the following challenges:

- DNAs (did not attend)
- Counselling only being available when students are actively enrolled on a course
- Meeting the hours required for trainee counsellors
- Students being referred against their wishes
- Restricting the number of sessions available
- Holidays disrupting the therapeutic flow of the counselling relationship.

10. Helplessness with regard to practical issues

Working with students can result in a range of issues presenting themselves. Often we can find ourselves in a place where our client is overwhelmed by their circumstances such as with debt, housing, childcare, travel expenses or their safety. Here we hear from Jane again and areas that she has come across in relation to a client's practical dilemmas:

- Lone working
- Being used as a crisis intervention service
- A pervading sense of hopelessness amongst adult learners following basic skills courses who worry that they are unemployable
- The current situation from a welfare perspective – cuts in benefits making family life extraordinarily strained
- Students finding it hard to hold on to hope for the future
- The impossibility of therapeutic work for individuals who are overwhelmed by anxiety caused by their situation.

To illustrate this, Jane provides an example of a situation with a client, Tanya, whose needs straddled the practical and the psychological. She was placed in a position where she had to prioritise the client's immediate needs before moving on to her additional issues.

Voices

Jane

'Tanya was referred to the College Counselling Service having broken down in tears in the classroom. Her teacher had been concerned about her for some time as she was a very committed student but often looked tired and distracted and her self-care had noticeably deteriorated over a period of months. She presented to the Service and told me that she could no longer cope with the stress that she was under. She was a mature student with four children of her own and was looking after two of her sister's children while her sister was unable to care for them. She was studying a vocational course that she hoped would lead to future employment. Alongside studying and caring for six children, she worked a few hours in a fast food restaurant and her partner worked part-time in a supermarket. They are both on a low income but managed to make ends meet – just about – until the changes to Working Tax Credit in April 2012. As the combined working hours for the couple was under 24 hours and neither worked as much as 16 hours they lost their Working Tax Credit. Both asked their employers for more hours but were not given enough. Losing the tax credit was catastrophic and the family was pushed deeply into poverty. Tanya had studied for a year and a half and did not want to drop out of her course when she only had six months more to do to achieve the qualification that would make her more employable. She found that she was not able to stretch the money far enough to feed the children all week and was hugely distressed having to put the children to bed while they were crying because they were hungry. She took them to school without packed lunches when she could no longer afford to give them food and would drop them on the street corner and run, being too ashamed to face the school when they would ask why the children did not have food. The situation came to a head when she was called into the school because her eleven-year-old son had been caught stealing a mobile phone. The school's policy was to call the police and she attended while they reprimanded him. She was utterly ashamed and devastated, but felt even worse when she walked him home and he cried saying that he had done it so that he could sell the phone and give her the money to *buy food. Her relationship with her partner had been under tremendous strain because of the financial difficulties and she was very concerned that they would separate. She was not sure that she would be able to cope alone. She said that she felt like taking all the children to Social Services and leaving them there as she felt that she was empty and not able to give them anything.*

'The challenges that I faced in dealing with this client were numerous. There was a very real welfare need so I referred her to our Welfare Advisor (one of the benefits of working in a multi-disciplinary team) who was able to refer her to a food bank. This was of immediate but not substantial ongoing support. I felt that it did something to help me to manage the anxiety that overwhelmed me as I heard her story. The desperation was palpable as was how precarious everything in her life felt: the survival of her family and her capacity to parent. The possibility of her managing her situation sufficiently to be able to engage in her studies seemed beyond hope. However, she considered the College to be her lifeline. She was not able to talk or cry with anyone else and the small window that the service gave her helped her to contain her anxiety. She spoke about the course as being the opportunity that she had waited for all her life and she clung on to it knowing that it represented a way out of her situation. She was continually in trouble on the course for handing assignments in late and not having the right equipment. She did not want the teaching staff to know about her situation so I respected her wishes and it remained confidential.'

From this vignette, we can see that Jane felt very conscious of the physical needs of Tanya and overwhelmed by her story. She recognised Tanya's motivations and her very real difficulties with regard to money and food. She also recognised the need for confidentiality and privacy. We can see that for Tanya her learning experience is seriously affected by her current home life; her financial situation, her role as a mother, her relationship, her shame and her feelings of not being able to cope. In this situation, attending counselling resulted in practical and emotional support. The counsellor was able to access immediate help from within her team to temporarily address an immediate issue. The client had a safe place to discuss her situation. This is a good example of clients that we may encounter and the range of challenges we face in balancing meeting their needs and also feeling that, professionally, we have done all that we can.

> ## Points to consider
> - Do you focus on the wellbeing of your client or their success on their course, or have you found a balance of both?
> - How do you respond to DNAs? Do you see the client who does not attend as a problem or as an indicator that there is a problem?

Further reading

BACP: U&C Special Interest Group (2008) 'Services Under Threat: A BACP: U&C Discussion Document'. *BACP: U&C Journal*. Lutterworth: BACP.

Balestra (2012) 'Challenges in Working with Hard-to-Reach Students in Further Education'. *AUCC Journal*. Lutterworth: BACP.

Bell, E. (1996) *Counselling in Further and Higher Education*. Buckingham: Open University Press.

Benson, N. (2007) 'Staff Counselling at the Interface: Working Creatively and Flexibly with the Organisation'. *AUCC Journal*. Lutterworth: BACP.

Coate, M. (2010) 'Guidance of Trainee Placements'. *T3 Information Sheet*. Lutterworth: BACP.

Hodgson, A. (2009) 'Auditing a Small Counselling Service'. *AUCC Journal*. Lutterworth: BACP.

Hodgson, A. (2008) 'Challenges for Staff'. *AUCC Journal*. Lutterworth: BACP.

Hodgson, A. (2005) 'Setting up a Staff Counselling Service'. *AUCC Journal*. Rugby: BACP.

Lawton, B., Bradley, A., Collins, J., Holt, C. & Kelly, F. (2010) *AUCC Guidelines for University and College Counselling Services* (2nd edn). Lutterworth: BACP.

Noonan, E. (1983) *Counselling Young People*. London: Routledge.

Reference

Reeves, A. (2013) *Challenges in Counselling: Self-harm*. London: Hodder Education.

Chapter 5
Strategies

In the previous chapter we identified and considered ten core challenges that counsellors face, working within educational settings. Here we will consider strategies to manage these anxieties. Much research has been completed in this area so we will integrate the discussions and findings that have been, or are currently, circulating around these issues. In addition to this, we will take into account suggested techniques, guidance regarding specific situations and sources of help that we can use to reduce our immediate concerns. Please do not view these as definite answers to situations but rather as a first step in the deliberation process when deciding what to do.

1. Financial constraints on counselling services

The challenges surrounding funding can be viewed as a single issue and tackled as such or more realistically, considered within the context of each area or incident. Firstly, the essential cost of staffing. We know from several national studies conducted by **BACP: U&C** that there are vastly varying approaches and models used to provide counselling services. We may feel that services that are well established and employ a team of counsellors, mental health advisors, nurses and welfare officers are lucky in that staff members are able to support each other. However, the financial challenges here are often greater as the costs will be considerable, making the service more visible to those responsible for reducing organisational spending. The other end of the scale also comes with distinct challenges where we find lone workers are responsible and often untrained to deal with budgeting requirements or services that rely heavily on volunteers and student placements (previously referred to as associate counsellors) with the belief that offering counselling by trainees is better than offering no counselling at all.

The issue of whether counsellors are employed full-time, part-time or as volunteers comes down to the constraints and ethos of the college or university. If counselling is viewed as important (and produces positive results), it warrants a budget. Logically, the size of the budget tends to equate to the size of the institution, so large university populations attract greater financial resources than small community-based centres. The staffing model within these centres then depends upon the autonomy and the approach of the manager. Offering post-qualified volunteers opportunities to build the hours necessary for their accreditation is a compromise many services make as although the counsellor may not be experienced, they have successfully completed their training and are very focused on their professional standards to gain their accreditation. In an ideal world, trainee placements should not replace paid counsellors in the same way that trainee nurses should not replace trained staff on a hospital ward. However, we have to accept that there are small counselling services that rely heavily (if not entirely) on trainee input. This can be managed with significant input by the trainees' course placement organiser, stringent counselling supervision and a supportive relationship with the counselling service provider. It would be irresponsible to deny that the provision of placements is crucial for both parties in this situation and the strict adherence to ethical guidelines.

As for other aspects of the service that require materials or resources, many services find that they do not have much, if any, say in the matter. Publicity may be provided in line with corporate procedures, furniture may be sourced from other departments and the counselling rooms or offices may be located in an area that no other department wants. It is the lucky few who have freedom to choose how they fund essentials.

2. Working with hard-to-reach students

Before we examine this area, I think it is important to state that a did not attend (**DNA**) is not always a bad thing! Below you will see that one counsellor uses the time available during a DNA session to catch up with paperwork.

Voices
• •

Jane

'Another difficulty [. . .] has been the relatively high rate of
DNAs that we have. I manage this by booking appointments
throughout the day on the assumption that not all will attend.
Invariably a few will not and this gives me time for writing
notes, service administration and lunch! I try very hard to select
highly motivated and committed clients to give to our trainees
but find that even these can and will DNA sessions. This can
be hugely frustrating for the trainees and can undermine their
confidence if not handled carefully.'

Figure 5.1 Did not attend

We have already recognised that there are many issues that can result in a
student presenting as a hard-to-reach client or as a DNA. Our decision now
is whether we fixate on the negatives and perceive DNAs as a poor reflection
of our own abilities or blame clients for being thoughtless, disrespectful of
our time and not valuing our sessions. Alternatively, we might reflect on the
reasons that lie behind the client not attending and use the insight in a positive framework to understand what the client is communicating through their
actions and how we can use that information to further develop our practice.

Counselling services monitor DNA rates and include them in their annual
evaluation. As a result of significant waiting lists and pressure to be seen
to be working to capacity, strategies are adopted to reduce the frequency
of DNAs.

Voices

Heidi

'The college staff recognised the high rate of DNAs and I believe did everything they could to try to address this including meeting with students before their first counselling session to ascertain whether they were coming to counselling voluntarily or via a tutor's instruction. They also emailed/ texted the student before their session to remind them of their appointment. Despite this, some students still failed to show up and unfortunately I think this may just be due to their age and their attitude towards college in general. Other students failed to turn up because their mental health problems impaired their ability to function on a daily basis.'

In my college counselling service, we had a DNA rate of 16 per cent last year. The national DNA rate averages from 7 per cent to 34 per cent in universities (but there are not currently equivalent figures available for colleges). Our administrator sends a text to clients 15 minutes prior to a session as a reminder. If they do not attend, she sends another text checking that they are OK and asking if they would like to make another appointment. (After two DNAs we no longer contact the client except by email for feedback on the service). (CORE, 2010)

3. Counselling staff and students

There are four key areas that can cause difficulties if a service is aiming to provide counselling for both students and staff. These are:

- Environment
- Boundaries
- Funding
- Management.

Environment

It is usual for staff and student counselling services to be either located in different areas or to have a different access point to reduce if not prevent clients meeting each other. Staff counselling may be based in the locale of the Human Resources (HR) department or an area that students do not have access to. If a client feels that there may be a conflict of interest in the location of the counselling service, most counsellors will attempt to accommodate the session elsewhere. I should point out here that this should go for any counselling service where the aim is to reduce the chance of any client feeling publicly visible or lacking privacy.

Boundaries

Larger staff counselling services may have the luxury of employing a different team of counsellors to prevent any potential overlap of boundaries. However, in smaller services this is unlikely to be possible. It may be that when allocating clients, counsellors concentrate on either one client group or the other, but if the team is so small that this is not possible, using an Employee Assistance Programme (**EAP**), where an external counselling service is bought in, might be the solution. This brings its own barriers as staff are often fearful of approaching their HR department to access counselling in case they are judged as not coping in some way. This can also be an expensive option for a small organisation. A compromise adopted by some services is to employ a part-time staff counsellor and offer an EAP service as well. This then offers a choice to staff as they can access in-house or external counselling.

As with student counselling services, there can be a dilemma surrounding the disclosure of clients attending the service. Often, staff choose to attend in-house counselling so they do not have to approach HR. The counselling service still needs to demonstrate how busy they are but in a way that does not break confidentiality and so aim to avoid identifying clients.

Funding

The funding of counselling services tends to be far from straightforward, so juggling different income sources is often par for the course. In general, institutions are far quicker to recognise the value of providing counselling as part of student support services but are often less convinced of the efficacy and cost of providing in-house staff counselling. Many institutions that do provide staff counselling do so in a slightly less structured manner than student counselling as a result from the lack of distinct funding for this service. Drop-in services or single-session meetings are more common, as is a referral service to external agencies for staff.

Management

The question of who oversees the service can be problematic. If a staff counselling service is provided as an add-on to the students' service, there is less of an issue as it is managed within a single structure. However, if the staff provision is a discrete service, it can be managed as a separate team, which can reduce communication between counsellors and precipitate divisions. This is an example of when sharing an office space has advantages if it results in the coming together of two counselling teams and encourages a single identity.

In 2005, Angela Hodgson published a very clear list of considerations as a guide when setting up a counselling service for staff. This is divided into ten sections that cover a wide range of issues from establishing a need for the service, the professional and environmental requirements, through to the service's relationship within the institution and how it may be further developed.

4. Relationship between counselling and academic outcomes

Most counselling services approach the challenge of balancing the emotional or psychological wellbeing of their students with the management's focus on success and retention by adopting a holistic view. Statistics are gathered, monitored and evaluated on a range of areas by the service, which addresses both areas. By this I mean that the counsellors may use an outcome measure such as **CORE-OM** (Clinical Outcomes in Routine Evaluation; a generic psychological measurement tool that is widely used to monitor client progress) to record the impact of the service on their clients which goes some way to demonstrate the impact of their counselling. In addition to this, other aspects of the service are measured which can be used to reinforce our value in relation to the educational outcomes and justify our existence. These figures may be gathered weekly, monthly or per academic year. Every service may differ but an example of the data collated includes:

- Enquiries or referrals to the service
- Sources of referral, for example, self, teaching staff, colleague, GP, courts, social workers, psychiatrists
- Appointments made
- Unaccommodated appointments

- Appointments cancelled by client (could not attend – **CNA**)
- Appointments cancelled by counselling service
- Appointments where client did not attend (DNA) or 'no show'.
- Average number of sessions that students attend
- Total number of counselling sessions delivered within the academic year
- The percentage attendance rate
- Gender balance of clients attending
- Age range of clients attending
- Waiting lists and times (between initial referral and assessment and between referral and first counselling session).

In addition to this, we may record additional information such as the variety of counselling approaches that are available or used, the number of placements offered to trainees or feedback from clients on the impact of attending counselling on themselves and their studies. However, there are ongoing discussions as to where our boundaries lie here in relation to confidentiality, in particular, when we disseminate our findings. We need to ensure that any information we are making available to external departments, such as management or funding bodies, does not compromise our ethical and professional standing. However the desire for transparency, honesty and the need to justify or reinforce our role can add more tension. This can be pre-empted to some extent in the care we take over our contracts with clients, ensuring that any signed contract includes careful detailing of information that may be requested by other sectors of the organisation.

5. Threat of outsourcing

When there is the risk of a service closing, due to not meeting the needs of the client population or management, this is uncomfortable but understandable. When a successful and well-used service is under threat because of budget cuts, it is easy for resentment and a sense of low esteem and value to grow. In relation to our therapeutic work we may feel that personal change is a constant and can be positive but we seem to find it harder to apply this to our environment and routine. This is linked to the perception of lack of control and disempowerment, but the process of having to reflect on justifying our practice, our service and our approaches to supporting students can actually be a positive experience. It challenges any complacency and stagnation, and encourages fresh and stimulating approaches. Understandably, this can be clouded by the fear of any consequences such as redundancy and downsizing or closure, but approaching the situation as we might a counselling session, the processes of risk-taking, change, self-questioning, honest reflection and development are healthy in relation to ourselves and the way we work. A practical guide to approaching this situation was published in the *AUCC Journal* in 2008, details of which can be found in the Further Reading section below.

6. Cultural issues

In Chapter 4 we considered how clients from different cultures may view and approach counselling. We have a professional and ethical responsibility to provide a safe space for them to explore their world; one where they do not feel judged or made to feel different in some way. To do this we must ensure that we are ready, sufficiently trained and prepared for meeting with a client in a situation that may be new to them. The **BACP** ethical guidelines (2010) state that 'Variations in client needs and cultural diversity differences are often more easily understood and responded to in terms of values'. We also need to consider:

- **Supervision.** We need to have access to an experienced supervisor who is well acquainted with issues that can arise. It may be necessary to attend additional supervision if this does not fall within our current supervisor's area of expertise.
- **Continuing professional development (CPD).** Further developing our training to include working with diversity is always good practice but becomes crucial when we are working within an educational setting. It is highly unlikely nowadays that we will not have a client whose cultural background is different to our own.
- **Flexibility.** Many other cultures view boundaries very differently from ourselves. We should reflect on our own feelings about boundaries and how flexible they are able to be, before we become uncomfortable.
- **Boundaries.** Time-keeping, confidentiality, the giving of gifts and the equality of the counsellor–client relationship are all areas where we may experience challenges. A client who approaches counselling differently to ourselves is unlikely to be applying the same meaning to their actions as we might. Therefore, rather than taking offence or reading a meaning from actions that is not intended, we should use greater empathy and understanding of the client's conditions.

- **Updating world knowledge.** Understanding the cultural and political background of a client will in turn increase our understanding of their situation, decision-making, world view and personal context.
- **Avoiding stereotyping.** Recognising the uniqueness and distinctive characteristics of our clients and avoiding culturally-based assumptions will help promote a trusting and safe relationship. Rather than focusing on differences, we should be seeing this client as a unique individual as we would with any of our clients.
- **Preparedness.** Ensuring that we consider potential pitfalls, barriers and challenges in advance, preferably with our supervisor, will make us less likely to feel out of our depth or encounter unexpected situations.

7. New developments

In the section on the threat of outsourcing, we introduced the concept of viewing our practice in a similar way to a client viewing their progress. Embracing change and improvement, whether it be on a personal or an organisation level, may be viewed with suspicion initially but we can make a conscious choice as to how we approach it. Our counselling training may not have included methods other than individual therapy, but a great number of the skills we learned are transferrable. Whether we are engaging with clients online, via telephone or Skype, we can still work from a basis of our original counselling training as the methods of communication and the ways of being do not alter depending upon our method of engagement. Online sessions can be in real time where we sit at a computer at the same time as our clients, but are considered in practical rather than financial terms. It is less likely to be suggested as it takes the same amount of time and staffing as face-to-face sessions, so the advantages are in respect of increased access rather than as a cost saving solution. The introduction of email support is more likely as it is not in real time; a client emails the counsellor who replies during a set time during their working schedule; for example, a counselling department may reply to all emails on a Tuesday and Thursday between 3 p.m. and 5 p.m. This allows for engaging with more students and offering wider support whilst managing it within the current staff team. A counsellor can reply to several students within a 50-minute session which they might otherwise be working with one client.

Telephone support is also being considered by many counselling services, which may or may not include Voice Over Internet Protocol (VOIP) services such as Skype, Google Voice or FaceTime. Straightforward, one-to-one telephone counselling has been around for many years and is used most commonly in colleges and universities as a way of engaging with more students. For some, the idea of being able to receive counselling within their environment of choice is an attractive one. Clients can remain 'hidden' to maintain a level of privacy that they would not otherwise have when attending face-to-face counselling. Not being able to see our client can, for some counsellors, be a concern: how can we form a connection with a client we cannot see? To overcome this perceived barrier, we may be more comfortable using a method that overcomes this obstacle whilst still allowing remote access. This is where services such as Skype have advantages. Although we do not save time, clients can access the service from any geographical location in the world. This of course is a great advantage if we are working in a remote area, or students find it difficult to attend or have enrolled on distance learning courses. The provision of this service and the freedom it offers may also be appealing for students with disabilities.

Group work is a well-recognised therapeutic intervention. It allows us to engage with a greater number of clients during each session than one-to-one sessions. This is clearly attractive to service managers when collating statistics regarding client numbers. Groups can cover a wide range of issues, so all present shared experiences or fears which usually creates a sense of camaraderie such as in the case of anxiety, fear of exams or bullying. However, there are difficulties in that clients may be embarrassed if they are identified as attending by their peers. They may feel intimidated by the presence of other students or initially put off by not knowing who else might attend. We know that with younger students, the influence of their peers is of great importance and this shapes their decision-making to some extent. As long as these issues are considered and planned for, group work can be an alternative option for students. The number of members of the group will have an impact on the dynamics; Barnes et al (1999.37) suggest that for the group process to be therapeutic there need to be at least five members, the ideal is six to nine, and above nine the individual's therapeutic process reduces. Larger groups can still bring great benefits to members but the therapeutic process is different to that in a smaller group.

It is common to fear technology when we are not comfortable with new developments. Students work with technology more and more on their courses (using virtual learning environments, or **VLE**s) and electronic access to sources, for example Athens). It is not unreasonable for younger students in particular to be comfortable engaging with technological solutions to providing psychological support; they may not view it as so alien as older people might. Developments are taking place in this area very quickly and may provide solutions for issues we are not yet aware of. As long as we have appropriate equipment and suitable training, technology can make our lives significantly easier. Even updating from a paper to an electronic system can make managing a counselling service less onerous. There is, however, a downside which might involve lack of expertise, no budget available for necessary equipment, security issues (such as encryption) or slow connection speeds. A good working relationship with the IT support department can ease any difficulties.

If we are contemplating introducing new ways of working, we must not forget that all the ethical and legal implications still apply. Confidentiality, privacy, licensing agreements, limitations and boundaries are all crucial to the safety of our practice. How do we know who we are actually communicating with? How do we know they are who they say they are? By this I mean that we need to have very robust procedures in place for clients entering into the counselling process. How we maintain confidentiality when we do not have control of our contribution is another issue to consider; if we are emailing clients, we then lose control of the session content, the client can forward the session to friends or print it off to circulate if they so wish. We must bear this in mind when we are contracting so we review as many eventualities we can think of. It is useful here to take advice from a service that is already offering this method of counselling. Professional dialogues online are also very enlightening.

Finally, the upkeep of our professional training is necessary, not only in relation to our counselling practice but also with regard to updating us in new developments with our methods of engagement with clients. The section on **CPD** in Chapter 7 covers this in more detail.

8. Risk of harm

Working with clients who have disclosed situations involving harm may initially cause feelings of panic or not knowing what to do. We may also react with feelings of wanting to rescue, save or protect our client. As with the previous chapter, I am going to divide this issue into client-work and self-work.

When a client divulges a situation where they or someone else is in harm, what exactly are our responsibilities? From a legal perspective, Reeves states that:

'It is important to note that (. . .) in the UK, there is no statutory responsibility for counsellors to break confidentiality with clients who self-harm. Likewise, there is no statutory responsibility to break confidentiality if there are concerns regarding suicide potential, or indeed child protection.'

Reeves (2013)

But the legal requirements do not necessarily help us on a personal or therapeutic level. We need to feel prepared and confident in our response and to do this, we need to have a strategy in place for working with clients in danger.

Within this strategy we need to consider how we will respond to our client on an immediate, relational level. By this I mean not to respond with shock or revulsion but to be seen to accept the client and their narrative. Then we need to consider our actions and how we will assess the level of risk. Following the session, specific support and guidance should be sought from both our counselling supervisor and/or our line manager depending upon the appropriateness: our supervisor can advise us with regard to our practice whilst our line manager can guide us towards policies, procedures and protocols. We have to balance the risk from the client's perspective with our perspective and recognise that they are both valid. It is also important that we do not insist that the risk takes over as a core theme to the counselling but that the voice of the client is heard and accepted. This subject is discussed in far greater detail in *Challenges in Counselling: Self-harm* by Andrew Reeves.

When it comes to our own situation of risk, we might initially deny its validity. In this situation, our discussions with our supervisor are invaluable to help us gain perspective. We might also consider a reflective journal, discussions with colleagues and personal therapy as methods of support. The loss of objectivity can be a barrier to helping us identify and reduce our own health resulting in the 'keep calm and carry on' approach. Online forums are also a great source of support for counsellors, especially those working alone. The **BACP** have published fact sheets which are useful too when looking for specific input.

9. Time constraints and waiting lists

In Chapter 4, three counsellors identified a list of challenges surrounding time constraints and waiting lists, which were:

- DNAs
- Counselling only being available when students are actively enrolled on a course
- Meeting the hours required for trainee counsellors
- Students being referred against their wishes
- Restricting the number of sessions available
- Holidays disrupting the therapeutic flow of the counselling relationship.

Here we shall address each separately. We have already considered our approach to DNAs and how they need not always be labelled as problematic. However, in relation to restricted sessions and long waiting lists, they are more likely to be viewed as a waste of time. How services approach DNAs varies but tactics such as texting clients a reminder just before their session, emailing students a session confirmation or issuing appointment cards, are all worthy of consideration. We have little control over how clients view their appointments but we do have control over how we react to DNAs. As previously discussed, we may reflect on DNA rates to inform our practice. This raises questions such as 'Why didn't this client attend? What is going on in their life that might have prevented them from coming? Are they OK?'

The concern raised by a counsellor regarding a student whose mental health deteriorated to a point where they were asked to leave their course so were no longer eligible to access free counselling is a valid one. Raising the issue with our line manager and supervisor, considering referral procedures and maintaining alternative methods of communication with the client may all be ways of finding a solution that both the client and counsellor find satisfactory. However, maintaining these connections with former clients does take time and adds to our workload but the continuing care and support of the client is often raised as an issue of anxiety.

Counselling courses place expectations on trainees to acquire counselling practice. This can be a very real worry for student counsellors on placement and it is usual for trainees to secure more than one placement to increase their opportunity for counselling and potentially reduce the time it takes to accrue their hours. Waiting lists are a boon for trainees but only if their placement allows them to work with clients who are waiting for counselling and the clients are happy for their counselling to be provided by a trainee. Levels of professionalism, standard of service and the policy of the service with regard to trainees are key issues here. Staff on counselling courses are constantly looking to start working with new placement providers but counselling services that are under-staffed or working within restrictive time pressures often find it hard to balance the benefit of an extra counsellor with the time it takes to mentor and support a trainee. If the counselling course provides supervision and has an active liaison team, it can make for a good compromise.

In my service, we experienced students being referred to counselling by members of staff in the college. It wasn't until we evaluated our DNA rate at the end of the academic year and included the method of referral that we noticed a distinct correlation between students who did not self-refer and not attending their counselling sessions. Conversely, students who did self-refer were far more likely to attend. This led us to make the decision that we would only accept self-referrals. If a member of staff was sufficiently concerned about a student to suggest counselling (which the student tended to 'hear' as a punishment), we invited the student to come along for an informal chat. During that time, if they turned up, the counselling process was explained to them and they were offered the opportunity to self-refer or we could help them to access additional forms of support. This immediately had a very positive impact on our DNA rate and we found that attendance improved dramatically.

10. Helplessness with regard to practical issues

There can often appear to be a fine line drawn between Rogers' warm, unconditional caring for a client and the care that we can feel when working with a client who genuinely requires practical help. In Chapter 4 we heard Jane reflecting on her concerns when working with Tanya and how she felt she could support her in a way that addressed her practical needs (see also her experience with Yusuf in Chapter 6). She was able to hear their financial and safety needs and was able to access welfare assistance without breaking confidentiality as her area of working was lucky enough to have a Welfare Advisor as part of the Student Services team. On a very basic level, if we consider Maslow's rather well-known Hierarchy of Needs, it helps us to identify when the physical needs such as food or sleep or the safety needs such as privacy and security have to take precedence over the therapeutic relationship in the present moment. How difficult might it be for a client to focus on their emotional or psychological wellbeing when they are aware of needing life-sustaining help? We have an ethical duty towards the protection of our clients and this is a very real example of how this might present itself. We often say during our contracting with a new client that we may require to pass information on if we believe someone is at risk; here we have a good example of risk but it is due to the student's circumstances and environment. Sometimes to progress with the therapeutic work we need to first support our client with an internal or external referral. Internal referrals may be to colleagues within our support team, as Jane did with Tanya, but there may also be a need to access additional input from professional services. Although I am aware that contact details can and do change over time, the contact details below were correct at time of print and may help with finding a direction to turn to, especially if you are a lone worker and do not have a team to turn to for guidance.

Resources

Abuse

MASH (Men As Survivors Helpline): w. **http://www.survivorsuk.org** t. 0117 907 7100

RASASC (Rape And Sexual Abuse Support Centre) t. 0845 122 1331

Women's Aid: w. **http://www.womensaid.org.uk** t. 08457 023 468

Advice

Citizens Advice Bureau: w. **http://www.adviceguide.org.uk** (separate national telephone numbers available on website)

Anxiety states

No Panic: w. **http://www.nopanic.org.uk** t. 0800 783 1531

Counselling

Confidential Care: t. 0800 281054 (24-hour)

Culturally specific assistance

Lifeline: (Christian Helpline) w. **http://www.premier.org.uk/life/lifeline/contact.aspx** t. 0845 345 0707

Miyad: (Jewish crisis helpline) t. 0800 652 9249

Muslim Women's Helpline: t. 020 8904 8193

Muslim Youth Helpline: w. **http://www.myh.org.uk** t. 0808 808 2008

Depression

Students Against Depression: w. **http://studentsagainstdepression. org** (no telephone option)

Look OK Feel Crap: w. **http://www.lookokfeelcrap.org** t. 0808 802 2020

Disability

SKILL (National Bureau for Students with Disabilities): w. **http://www. skill.org.uk/youth/**

Dyslexia

British Dyslexia Association: w. **http://www.bdadyslexia.org.uk** t. 0118 966 8271

Discrimination

Equal Opportunities Commission: w. **http://www. equalityhumanrights.com** t. 0800 444 205

Eating disorders

Eating Disorders Association: w. **http://www.b-eat.co.uk** t. 0845 634 1414

General support for students.

The Student Room: w. **http://www.thestudentroom.co.uk** (no telephone option)

Nightline: w. **http://nightline.ac.uk/about-us** t. Click on 'Need to Talk?' to find a local number

HIV/AIDS

Terrence Higgins Trust: w. **http://www.tht.org.uk** t. 0845 1221 200

Listening service

Samaritans: w. **http://www.samaritans.org** t. 08457 90 90 90 (UK) or 1850 60 90 90 (ROI)

Loss and bereavement

Bereavement Advice Centre: w. **http://www.bereavementadvice.org** t: 0800 6349494

A Different Journey: w. **http://www.careforthefamily.org.uk** t: 029 20810800

If I Should Die: w. **http://www.ifishoulddie.co.uk**

Medical advice

National Sexual Health Helpline: t. 0800 567 123

NHS Direct: w. **http://www.nhsdirect.nhs.uk** t. 0845 46 47

Mental health

Saneline: w. **http://www.sane.org.uk** t. 0845 7678000

You and Your Mental Health: w. **http://www.rethink.org/young_people/index.html** (no telephone option)

Pregnancy and abortion

British Pregnancy Advisory Service: w. **http://www.bpas.org/bpaswoman** t. 08457 304 030

Search engine to locate services specialising in a range of issues in your local area

Get Connected: w. **http://search.getconnected.org.uk/GetConnected/Search.do** t. 0808 8084994

Sex and sexuality

EACH (Educational Action Challenging Homophobia): w. **http://www.eachaction.org.uk** t.0800 100 0143

Lesbian and Gay Switchboard: w. **http://www.llgs.org.uk** t. 0300 330 0630

Substance use

Alcoholics Anonymous: w. **http://www.alcoholics-anonymous.org.uk** t: 0845 7697 555

Alcohol Concern: w. **http://www.alcoholconcern.org.uk**

Drinkaware: w. **http://www.drinkaware.co.uk/** t. Drinkline 0800 9178282 (England & Wales)

Drink Smarter: w. **http://www.drinksmarter.org** t. Drinkline 0800 7314314 (Scotland)

National Drugs Helpline: t. 0800 77 66 00

NHS choices: w. **http://www.nhs.uk/livewell/alcohol/Pages/Alcoholhome.aspx**

Release: w. **http://release.org.uk** t. 020 77494034

Talk to Frank: w. **http://www.talktofrank.com** t. 0800 776600

Under-19-year-olds

Youth2Youth: w. **http://www.youth2youth.co.uk/index.htm** t. 020 88963675

Victims of crime

Victim Support line: w. **http://www.victimsupport.org** t. 0845 3030 900

When it comes to referrals to external agencies such as the NHS or a student's GP, there are some factors to consider. The NHS does not automatically consider academic holidays in the way that an in-house counselling service might, resulting in students possibly finding that their appointments are not convenient, especially if they fall outside term time. According to the 2011 *Mental Health of Students in Higher Education* report by the Royal College of Psychiatrists, there are four specific recommendations made to psychiatrists and the NHS to ensure they meet the needs of the student population in Higher Education:

1. National Health Service providers of mental healthcare are urged to recognise and respond to the particular mental health needs of the student population and the difficulties that many experience in gaining equal access to services.
2. Clinicians are strongly urged to give due regard to the needs and vulnerabilities of patients with mental disorders who are embarking on higher education for the first time.
3. Students often benefit significantly by being able to gain access to dedicated student health services.
4. The Royal College of Psychiatrists should consider the establishment of a student mental health special interest group, which could provide a forum for the development of services and research.

And five recommendations for Higher Educational establishments:

1. We recommend that this provision, which greatly enhances the student experience, be maintained and, when possible, expanded.
2. We recommend that all higher education institutions give careful consideration to enhancing the academic and personal support available to mentally troubled students.
3. It is recommended that all higher education institutions have a formal mental health policy.
4. It is recommended that higher education institutions consider the adverse impact of alcohol misuse in students.
5. The 'Healthy Universities' systemic and holistic approach is commended and should be adopted as widely as possible.

The report recommends that all sectors take heed of the following:

- Higher education institutions and NHS psychiatric services who provide care to students should establish some form of coordinated working relationship.

- There would also be benefit from closer collaboration between higher education institutions and the NHS with regard to the formulation of local and national policies in relation to the mental wellbeing of students.
- All sectors are encouraged to recognise and pay attention to the needs of particularly vulnerable subgroups such as international students and students with a history of mental disorder.
- There is a need for systematic, longitudinal research into the changing prevalence over time of mental disorders in students. We need to know more about academic and social outcomes in students who go to university with pre-existing psychiatric illnesses.
- Rates of treatment uptake have been found to be low in some studies of student populations. There is a need to identify the reasons for this and where possible take remedial action.

One of the areas highlighted by the Mental Well-Being in Higher Education (**MWBHE**) is that of continuity of care to ensure that students are supported by the university in a manner that complements their ongoing medical care. The MWBHE website provides links to their guidelines and research findings which can be of help when working in Higher Education and considering how we might support students with diagnosed mental health conditions. Further information about this working group can be found at **http://www.mwbhe.com**.

Summary

- Providing placements for associate counsellors can be a good way of increasing provision providing supervision and support are in place.
- DNAs are not always bad – they can be used to catch up with paperwork and can help us to reflect on our practice.
- Counselling services that cater for both staff and students have an additional set of challenges.

Further reading

AUCC (2007) Annual Survey for Academic Year 2006–7. Available at **http://www.bacp.co.uk/admin/structure/files/repos/261_AUCC_ staff_counselling_survey_data_from_academic_year_2006-7_fe_ institutions.pdf** (accessed 15 October 2012).

AUCC Special Interest Group (2008) 'Services Under Threat: An AUCC Discussion Document'. *AUCC Journal*. Lutterworth: BACP.

Coate, M. (2010) 'Guidance of Trainee Placements'. *T3 Information Sheet.* Lutterworth: BACP.

Conlon, A. (2007) 'Know the Territory – An Overview of the UK Higher Educational Arena'. *AUCC Journal.* March 2007, pp. 13–20.

CORE: Clinical outcomes in routine evaluation. Benchmarks for higher education counselling services: Sessions attended/unattended, n9, July 2010, cited by Balestra, E. Challenges in working with hard-to-reach students in further education. *AUCC Journal*, May 2012: 20.

Hodgson, A. (2005) 'Setting up a Staff Counselling Service'. *AUCC Journal.* Lutterworth: BACP.

Nelson, H. (2006) 'Staff Counselling Models of Provision'. *AUCC Journal.* August 2006, pp. 18–21.

Royal College of Psychiatrists. (2011) *College Report CR166: Mental Health of Students in Higher Education.* London: RCPsych.

References

Barnes, B., Ernst, S. & Hyde, K. (1999) *An Introduction to Groupwork.* Hampshire: MacMillan.

Reeves, A. (2013) *Challenges in Counselling: Self-harm.* London: Hodder Education.

Chapter 6
Possible impact on clients

So far we have considered counselling from the practitioner's perspective but, of course, challenges are experienced very differently from the client's perspective. Specific issues which arise for the client such as stress, anger and anxiety can be challenging enough in counselling settings but here we need to bear in mind that our client's feelings can impede their studies which, in turn, can impact negatively on their feelings. This downward spiral can be incredibly draining for clients who are students. In this chapter we will consider why students may attend counselling, the impact that different aspects of a counselling service can have from the student's perspective, specific issues and finally, we will examine challenges within a longer case study.

Who are our clients?

Just as with any counselling service, we find that clients are unique; however, we also find that there are some commonalities, simply because of the sharing the experience of studying. I have considered some of the main groups that have attended our service over the years as a way of trying to identify the sheer range of experiences that can bring a student into education.

Adult returners
There are many reasons why adults may return to education following a gap but it is common to find students who are seconded from their work for continuing professional development (**CPD**) requirements, mothers who have brought up a family and are looking to re-enter the workforce, those who have been made redundant and wish to retrain and students who are attending out of personal interest in a particular subject area.

School leavers

Both universities and colleges attract a significant number of school leavers. It is hard not to generalise here but often if they were successful at school they will attend university to obtain a degree or college to train in a specialist vocation. Alternatively, school leavers who did not achieve academic success are likely to attend college for financial reasons, such as to receive a bursary. We have found that this age group (16–24 years) is by far the greatest population who request counselling.

Slightly differently to the above are students who are not school leavers but who had a poor school experience when they did attend, and often find studying stressful. Jane, working in **FE**, shares this experience:

Voices

Jane

'I have seen a lot of adults who are coming through functional skills training in order to hold on to jobs that previously had not required such skills. For example, in childcare/childminding or care assistants, these posts now involve a much higher level of literacy, as written records are required. This has forced a considerable number of students on to courses with high anxiety about the implications of failure. My belief is that there are always significant reasons why a person without a learning disability reaches adulthood without basic literacy and numeracy. My experience has been that there is often a history of trauma or considerable deprivation that impacted upon their capacity to learn as children. The inheritance of these experiences must be acknowledged and worked through for learning to be possible in adulthood.'

Those with a positive school experience

This sector of the student population are less likely to present with issues surrounding their studies but are just as prone to personal issues as anyone else.

- We find that many students who have newly left home request counselling. Some of their issues may involve the radical change in their lifestyle and struggles with new-found independence.

- International students, whether being funded by their family, seeking asylum or emigrating, can bring enormous cultural change and possible isolation.
- Students who are filling in time because they cannot find employment. This can be a massively frustrating and unfortunately all too common situation where their heart is not really in their studies as it is not where they really want to be.

Government initiatives, such as modern apprenticeships, attract students into education.

The impact of different aspects of the counselling service

We can see from this list that our clients can come from all age groups and from all walks of life. For that reason, we have to make sure that we consider the impact that different aspects of our counselling service can have upon them and ensure that we are as inclusive and as accessible as possible.

Theories and skills

In Chapter 3 we considered a range of theories and skills that we might find useful working with this client group. If we are skilful and develop a receptive and therapeutic relationship, our training and theoretical underpinning might be almost invisible to our client. If, however, we are unsure of what we are doing, hesitant or lacking in confidence, our client may be increasingly aware of it. Research suggests that the relationship and process we have with our client is just as important if not more so than the theory we use (Cooper, 2008; Wampold 2001:11, 26, 2008). Therefore to benefit from this, we should focus on:

- a sound underpinning theoretical base
- an appropriate counselling process
- use of relevant skills, and
- a warm and welcoming manner.

It makes sense that if our client likes us, they are more likely to return (Piper *et al*, 1999). Our choice of theory will be determined by our training and qualifications as well as our value base and world view. In addition to this, our use of skills will develop over time depending upon our experiences with clients and our **CPD**. The combination of this is intended to reassure the client, do no harm and heighten the chance of a positive outcome.

Confidentiality

Although we may be confident with our confidentiality policy and aware of the privacy that we strive for within our service, students might not. Clients who have never attended counselling before may have their own understanding of confidentiality based on hearsay or the internet. Clients who have attended counselling before but within the statutory sector may expect a sharing of information between the staff team. We have to be very clear when we explain our policy to ensure our client is left in no doubt about who has access to their information. This includes written notes, computer records, attendance records and any discussions that include the session content. Some ethical issues surrounding confidentiality are examined further in Chapter 8.

Environment and privacy

The placing of the service can have an undeniable impact on how comfortable or uncomfortable a student may feel about attending. Counselling rooms that are in a secluded area may feel more private but are not ideal if the department is labelled clearly with 'COUNSELLING SERVICE'. Finding the balance can be challenging, which I discovered when asking students about where on the campus they would feel most comfortable attending. Interestingly, we found that having our counselling rooms placed in a very central and yet totally anonymous area was surprisingly popular. Despite being in the reception area, passing students were completely unaware that counselling was taking place as the interview rooms were unlabelled, private and used by many different services. When the counselling service was allocated a dedicated (but unlabelled) room within student services, it became more apparent to staff but not to other students. We made sure that our counselling room has two doors so that a client might enter or exit from a different door if they so choose. Soundproofing can also be an issue which some services counter by playing music quietly in the corridor area to lessen the chance of voices being heard outside the counselling room.

Information and marketing

The use of a website and leaflets are common, and the 'tone' that services use in their marketing is important. Finding the balance between being professional but not overly clinical, welcoming without being inappropriately interfering can be challenging. Students need to know what is available without feeling patronised or medicalised.

Warm welcome

The welcome a client receives when they first enter the counselling service gives the first impression of the service resulting in the client feeling comfortable and relaxed or an unexpected nuisance. A private seating area, a calm atmosphere with an understanding, patient and friendly receptionist make a big difference to the clients' experience.

Attendance

We are encouraged in our training to be reflective but sometimes this can develop into becoming self-critical. When a client fails to attend a session it is very easy to first ask ourselves *'Why haven't they come back? What did I do wrong?'*. When clients who **DNA** are contacted by the service administrator, it is surprising how many clients apologise for not turning up saying, 'I feel better now, it was really good to get it all off my chest. I'll make another appointment if I need one'. We have found this is particularly common with younger clients, even if they have discussed and agreed to a series of sessions during their initial contracting.

Voices

Heidi

'Some clients only came once or twice, so it is hard to know what the impact of counselling was on them. Other clients who stayed longer were often happy to tell me how counselling was benefiting them. I have been told by clients that they feel "more understood" and have made comments such as "I feel less alone with this"; "I don't feel like I'm going mad anymore"; "I understand myself more" and "My problems are still there but I think I can deal with them better now".

'I feel that if students are asked to leave the course, support in these circumstances should be extended. Despite the fact that the student is no longer registered on the course, this can be a particularly stressful and upsetting time for them and their welfare must be considered. A further amount of sessions could be offered to the client, say three or four, enabling them to work towards a more satisfactory ending. During this time the counsellor can help signpost other support if the client feels he still needs it.'

Figure 6.1 I understand myself more

In your experience, what has been the impact of counselling on your clients?

Voices

Jane

'I am convinced that counselling has a profound impact on many of the service users, feedback both formally and informally has attested to this – that clients feel that they may well have not completed or been successful in their courses if they had not had counselling. In some cases I believe that it has helped hold families together and has even been life-saving.'

What can be challenging?

Voices

Heidi

'From my own experiences and from what I have learned from my clients, I would suggest that financial pressures can be overwhelming and very worrying for some students. Time

> *management can be a challenge; juggling a social life, study, work, childcare and home responsibilities. There is also a lot of pressure to succeed; constant assessments and assignments mean constant judgements are made with regard to the students. This can either increase or decrease their self-esteem depending on the outcome.'*

The focus here is on what our clients, the students, find challenging. Studying is rarely easy, it is not designed to be, or courses would lack value. So being under pressure to perform academically or creatively can be stressful. We touched briefly on student issues in Chapter 2, but here are a range of issues that can arise for students in all sorts of areas. The categories of key concerns have been identified by the **AUCC** (2009):

Abuse	Physical, emotional, sexual, financial, institutional and neglect
Academic	Assessments, exam stress, dyslexia, fear of failure
Addictive behaviour	Substances, behaviours, compulsions, dependencies
Anxiety	Fear, panic, stress, worry, phobias
Depression, anger and mood change or disorder	Mood swings, anger issues
Eating disorders	Controlled and uncontrolled eating, compulsions
Loss	People, things, situations
Other mental health conditions	Diagnosed and undiagnosed
Physical health	Injury, illness, disability
Relationships	Family, friends, intimacy, sexuality, loneliness
Self-harm	Intentional, unintentional, suicide
Self and identity	Esteem, culture, achievement
Sexual issues	Pregnancy, abortion, infection
Transitions	Roles, homesickness, status
Welfare and employment	Un/employment, legal issues, time constraints, stress

Table 6.1 Student issues

We can see from this list that there is a considerable range of issues that clients might bring to our sessions. Many might appear within any setting but there are others that are specific to education that we have a professional responsibility to learn more about. These are general areas of concern but within these, clients can experience very specific issues such as anxiety attacks, insomnia at times of assessments/exams, peer problems, tutor problems within the college, a poor study environment at home and the subsequent impact on college work or financial hardship. How we work through these with our client, will have an effect on their comfort in further disclosure.

Distance learning

When attendance is optional, a student may never meet fellow students or tutors, so a sense of isolation may well set in. How students manage this without seeking face-to-face support was investigated in a study involving adult returners engaging in distance learning for their employment. Dearnley (2003) monitored nurses retraining and identified three main areas in which they gained support during their course:

1. *academic* support from tutors and peers;
2. *professional* support by colleagues, managers and mentors; and
3. *social* support of partners, children, extended families and friends.

These three aspects took on a pivotal role in determining whether the students were able to manage on the course. It is clear that if a student isn't able to access these and no offer of additional support is forthcoming, the retention rate of a course may fall significantly.

Finance and time

The access, provision and availability of counselling all depend upon funding, time and expertise being available to offer counselling to students. Jane acknowledges this:

Voices

Jane

'Central to the role of counselling in an educational setting is enabling the students to remain on course and to complete successfully. This often creates tensions when clients are

> *unable to learn and it can be difficult to balance the frustration of the organisation – not wanting to "waste" resources on people who are not going to be successful, and concentrating on the needs of the client. Their circumstances can be overwhelming.'*

One of our challenges as service providers might be **DNA**s but from a client's perspective, the ability to attend or not is important. As with most services, clients appreciate flexibility; how we manage that can be challenging. Sticking to scheduled sessions at the same time every week might be easier administratively but a client might prefer to choose their next appointment time on a week-by-week basis. Finding a balance that works is not easy but improves the client's experience and ultimately lowers **DNA** rates.

What might be challenges for the client?

This is a case study of a client that Jane worked with. We can see as we read this, that many issues are raised both for Yusuf and for Jane that were particularly challenging:

Case study

Yusuf was a 17-year-old from Iraq. He came to the UK as an unaccompanied minor at 15 years old following the murder of his parents in Iraq. He was accommodated in a foster family until his sixteenth birthday then moved to semi-supported accommodation that consisted of a room in a house filled with other asylum seekers. His asylum claim was rejected and he was given discretionary leave to remain until his eighteenth birthday. He presented to the Counselling Service after disclosing to his tutor that he was afraid at his home because the other residents were from another culture and spoke a language that he did not understand. He said that they made him feel uncomfortable and unwelcome. He avoided sleeping because of the nightmares that he had every night. He had woken screaming several nights in a row and the other residents were angry with him for waking them. He had taken to riding night buses to keep out of their way and to try to stay awake. He was clearly very vulnerable. Through counselling it became evident that he was deeply traumatised by the events that preceded his escape from Iraq. His major preoccupation was the loss of security in being able to stay in the UK. It felt as though he was in too precarious a position to even begin to look at the past or to the future when he was constantly aware that each day brought him closer to the possibility of deportation. He was terrified of being sent back, knowing that there was no surviving family to go to and no infrastructure to support him. His attendance at college was erratic and he often struggled to stay awake in class.

Activity

- What specific issues can you identify that Yusuf was experiencing?
- What challenges are there for Jane?
- How do you think Jane might work with Yusuf to overcome these issues?

This is what Jane actually did:

'As I sat with Yusuf and he repeatedly asked what I could do for him, I stumbled over an explanation of counselling that felt utterly woolly in the context of what he was facing. He tried to be polite to me but said that he could not see the point in talking about his situation if I couldn't give him advice or change things for him. I was reminded of Maslow's Hierarchy of Needs and asked myself if there was any point in seeing a client whose basic needs of safety and security were not met. I tried hard to hold on to the belief that the therapeutic space was valuable and that if I held my own anxiety in check and maintained the boundaries for him that he would find a use for it. We had a number of sessions where he raged against me for not being useful to him, but he kept on coming and I believed that there was a message to me in that. I decided to make a disclosure, which is very unusual for me as I rarely do. I had a sense that he felt that I was withholding something from him and he could not understand why I would do that.

He repeated again that he did not want to talk about the past and what had happened in Iraq, he wanted to focus on how to live in the present. He respectfully referred to my age and how I could guide him with the knowledge I have about the world. I told him about a time when I was at university and had had a terrible year, I did not go into any detail about what had happened but did say that it had impacted upon me greatly, I was deeply unhappy and found focusing on my work almost impossible. This came to a head at exam time and I went to the counselling service, wanting to unburden myself but not knowing how to. I gave my presenting issue as anxiety about the forthcoming exams. The counsellor did not take time to get to know me or to ask about my life in general, but stepped straight into advising me on study techniques and breathing for anxiety. I went away feeling utterly unmet and with a sense that she was neither interested in me nor able to offer anything useful. I told Yusuf that I needed to get to know him to understand who he is, then we can look together at what he needs. He understood instantly and relaxed into telling me his story in detail. I was aware that he had told his story to many people, immigration officials, solicitors, social workers, and could understand his reluctance to talk to someone else. He needed to know why he was telling it, what I would do with it and what the purpose was for our meeting. He continued to make great use of this space.'

Impact on Jane	Impact on Yusuf
She felt 'woolly'	He felt he was wasting his time
Unable to give advice or change things for him	Unsure of purpose of sessions
Questioning herself	Kept attending
Concerned regarding his safety	Wanted advice, change, wisdom
Unsure of value of sessions	Wanted to focus on future rather than past
Self-disclosure	Feeling of shared understanding
Feeling of breakthrough/ progress	Feeling of breakthrough/progress

Table 6.2 Comparison of personal experience

We can see from Jane's response that the impact of counselling on Yusuf was very different to her own experience as counsellor in two key ways. Firstly her self-disclosure illustrated a very different history to his, and secondly, her feelings, thoughts and reactions during the session demonstrated a divergence. However, she was sufficiently skilled to take an educated risk in an approach she would not normally use which was what was needed for a successful connection to be made.

Summary

- Our client's experience will always be different from our own
- Our clients come from all walks of life and can't be stereotyped
- The relationship we develop is the most important aspect of our therapeutic alliance.

References

AUCC (2009) *Categories of Client Concern* (3rd edn). Available at **http://www.AUCC.uk.com/Members_Area/index.php** (accessed 4 January 2013).

Cooper, M. (2008) *Essential Research Findings in Counselling and Psychotherapy: The facts are friendly.* London: Sage.

Dearnley, C. (2003) 'Student Support in Open Learning: Sustaining the Process'. *International Review of Research in Open and Distance Learning*, vol. 4(1).

Piper, W.E., Ogrodniczuk, J.S., Joyce, A.S., McCallum, M., Rosie, J.S., O'Kelly, J.G. & Steinberg, P.I. (1999) 'Prediction of dropping out in time-limited, interpretive individual psychotherapy'. *Psychotherapy: Theory, Research, Training.* 36(2):114–22.

Wampold, B.E. (2001) *The Great Psychotherapy Debate: Models, Methods and Findings.* Mahwah, NJ: Erlbaum.

Chapter 7
Professional issues

When it comes to professional issues such as supervision, employment and accreditation, there are many regulations that apply to each individual counselling service. These include specific guidelines such as policies and procedures, the service management structure, funding streams, the range of counselling qualifications and accrediting bodies. Rather than cover each possibility, which would make this chapter the length of the book itself, I felt it would be more helpful to contextualise the role and hear from counsellors already working to gain a glimpse of their professional experiences.

Continuing professional development

Continuing professional development (**CPD**) is a requirement of most professions. The **BACP** website states that:

'A responsible professional will use a framework of developmental, learning activities to enhance their effectiveness in and around their area of qualification and/or expertise.'

www.bacp.co.uk

In addition to our counselling practice and CPD (including theory and skills), in educational settings we adhere to a plethora of explicit legislation, which is continually being updated (safeguarding and equality to name but two) and work with university or college systems (such as IT) that are often updated. It is important to maintain current knowledge in all three of these areas to remain professional. Finding the time and the money to attend developmental events can be difficult, which is why such a range of CPD is considered valuable – even reading professional journals. All CPD activities (formal and informal) should be recorded in detail.

Complaints

Each counselling service should have their own complaints procedure that falls in line with both the institution's policies and the professional body that governs them. With smaller services such as lone workers, this should still be in place but may be less detailed than in larger teams. It is always a good idea to read the procedures of other services and be guided by your professional lead body to ensure your policy is comprehensive. Many services make their policies and procedures available online.

Assessment and risk

Before working therapeutically with students, we conduct an assessment. How this is carried out differs between services, varying from a brief introduction at the start of the first counselling session, through to a formal assessment process where the client is assigned appropriate support. During this process the counsellor and client share information; the counsellor providing information regarding the counselling provision and the client sharing information about themselves. We have a responsibility at this point to assess levels of risk, whether that be to the client, to their acquaintances or to ourselves. Some services have staff who specialise in assessing new clients, although guidance for this should have been covered within your counselling training or been provided by your line manager. Wheeler *et al* (2004) identified the need for counselling training courses to include:

- Opportunities for trainees to understand risk factors that can help inform an understanding of risk and can help shape the dialogue between the counsellor and client
- The continued integration into supervision training programmes of issues surrounding working with risk
- A higher profile for violence to others and its management within counsellor training
- Risk assessment to be included more explicitly in the accreditation of courses by **BACP**.

We should be comfortable with how we would deal with risk and might consider these questions:

- Do we have robust procedures in place?
- Is risk discussed with a line manager?
- When is risk taken to supervision?
- Is there a clear referral policy?
- How is the balance between risk and confidentiality maintained?

Accreditation

At the time of writing (2013), we do not have a mandatory registration or accreditation scheme in the UK, which results in counsellors with a range of levels of training and experience working in universities and colleges. Clearly there are advantages and disadvantages to this, depending upon whether you are a counsellor, manager or client and the arguments surrounding this issue may continue for years to come. We do not have room to investigate the general debate here so have identified some of the current organisations that counsellors commonly join below.

- British Association for Counselling and Psychotherapy (BACP) (**http://bacp.co.uk**)

The voluntary accreditation scheme that BACP manage is recognised as an industry standard due to the high level of professionalism involved. They are developing a Certificate of Practice (COP) scheme for members who do not meet the requirements of accreditation.

- Association for University and College Counselling (**AUCC**) (**http://www.aucc.uk.com**)

The AUCC is a division of BACP which researches, collates and disseminates counselling developments and practices in educational settings. They also offer support networks to their members and promote best practice through their journal, intranet and conferences.

- British Psychological Society (BPS) (**http://www.bps.org.uk**)

The British Psychological Society is the representative body for psychology and psychologists working in the UK. They offer a professional accreditation scheme as well as the monitoring, expansion, advancement and implementation of the use of psychology.

- Counselling and Psychotherapy Central Awarding Body (**CPCAB**) (**http://www.cpcab.co.uk**)

CPCAB is a nationally approved awarding body so it designs, offers, assesses and certificates counselling qualifications.

- Confederation of Scottish Counselling Agencies (**COSCA**) (**http://www.cosca.org.uk**)

A professional body in Scotland that develops, delivers and assesses counselling qualifications. They also have an accreditation scheme.

Referrals

Referral is a two-way process; students are referred to our counselling service (either self-referrals or by a third party) and there are occasions when we need to refer our clients to colleagues or outside agencies. This is one area where there seems to be much disparity between services. There is some logic in that the larger the organisation, the more structured and well-staffed the counselling service. However, there are many organisations where counselling is not an integrated department within the establishment, who only employ student placements or lone workers and that do not work with many clients. Heidi, a student placement, found this:

Voices

Heidi

'Referrals can sometimes be sparse, which is why I took on an extra placement. Between both colleges I managed to accrue enough client hours for my postgraduate diploma.'

The popularity of a counselling service determines how many sessions each counsellor conducts within a day which can vary from one to eight. Appropriate advertising of the service can increase client numbers (for example posters in student toilet cubicles). Having too many referrals can result in long waiting lists and losing potential clients who may drift away. Many services increase the number of student or associate counsellors to help. As for referring clients on, this depends very much on the client's situation and the relationship with the counsellor. It should be conducted with care as it is easy for a client to 'hear' referral as, 'My problem is so great, even my counsellor can't cope with it'.

Supervision

Attending professional supervision is a requirement of all counsellors and is clearly very important to Jane, Heidi and Elaine. Not all services provide in-house supervision or even fund external supervision for counsellors. It is often left up to the practitioner to arrange (and pay for) their own. Supervision needs can change over time, as Elaine found:

Voices

Elaine

'I can only speak from my experience when I reflect on my first year as a student counsellor to the present day and the range of clients I have counselled over those years. I feel very different being a qualified counsellor in the college setting, I feel I give more but I want more in return. I want a deeper level of supervision, as I grow and develop as a counsellor, my needs change; I want to discuss client work at a deeper level.'

Elaine also felt that there are times during the academic year when in-house supervision would be of particular support:

'Supervision on the last day of term would be a huge benefit to me. In my experience as a counsellor, we prepare ourselves mentally for all the bad experiences we hear about. I do small checks and have little rituals when preparing for endings in the counselling relationship between my client and I, which all works fine because endings are usually staggered in other work places. Then WHAM, last day of college, three clients all ending in a morning. The emotions I feel on that day are hard to contain, pure joy your client has made it to the end of the year, sadness your relationship is over and an eminent feeling of pride in these amazing individuals, and that piece of paper that says they have achieved something. BANG, the college door shuts behind you, where do I go with all these emotions? [There is an] overwhelming feeling of being kicked out of a warm, cosy house and being left freezing on a snowy doorstep. So yeah, I feel the need for supervision on the last day of term to share this joy and wonderment in a profession that is not as credited as it should be. I wish I could bottle some of the amazing experiences in a college counselling relationship.'

Jane explains how she has managed her supervision and suggests a possible solution:

Voices

Jane

'There has been a difficulty in resourcing it properly in that the boundary issues continue to exist if I supervise the trainee and am therefore party to information about my clients that they are not aware of. It has taken a significant amount of my own supervision time to explore these issues and hold the separate clients. The college would not finance external supervision for trainees who are only seeing a couple of clients each. I am located in a large city with other colleges within fairly close geographical distance. I have tried to set up reciprocal supervision arrangements, whereby I could provide supervision for their trainees and they provide it for ours, but have never managed to implement this.'

Even when supervision is offered, it is not always an ideal solution as Heidi discovered:

Voices

Heidi

'One of the colleges that I worked in offered monthly group supervision, but unfortunately I was only able to attend once due to it clashing with my day at university. I was offered one-to-one supervision instead. The other college, where I'm currently still volunteering, does not offer any kind of supervision.'

Figure 7.1 Lack of paid work

Employment status

We know by now that there is no continuity in the employment patterns of counselling services within universities and colleges; teams, lone workers, student placements, volunteers, and no provision at all are all prevalent. Here counsellors have contributed some of their feelings about their personal experiences. Elaine challenges the cyclic nature of the academic year for services that support student placements from her perspective:

Voices

Elaine

'So are colleges set to offer counselling up to a level
with no hope to excel because of voluntary and student
counsellors coming and going with no continuity? Why can't
there be a mix? In my ideal world there would be two part-
time permanent qualified counsellors and students, with a
supervisor to oversee. This would create an excellent team,
a solid structure to enable a safe and robust counselling unit
that is constantly growing and developing. This would create
more opportunity for supervision and care of counsellors,
there could be cover for holidays enabling the counselling
service to stay open during breaks, offering more continuity
for clients.'

On the other hand, Heidi, a student placement, has identified a benefit
to working within the academic year:

Voices

Heidi

'I understand that many of the universities employ therapists
to counsel students but there seem to be fewer opportunities
to gain paid employment through placements at colleges.
For me, volunteering at colleges both during my counselling
training and now I have qualified is very beneficial because of
the terms and holidays. I am a lone parent to a primary school-
aged child and would not be able to afford to pay for childcare
during the holidays for voluntary work.'

For Jane, as an employed counsellor, working with students has been a
positive experience:

Voices

Jane

'Placements, running a placement scheme for trainees has been a another aspect of my work that I enjoy and feel challenged by. The incentive for the college was the ability to extend our service at low cost. I enjoy working with trainees, and doing supervisor training was great CPD for me. [When I was a lone worker, I found that] there are many benefits to working alongside trainees, for example, in common with many counsellors in FE I have been a lone practitioner. This can often lead to complicated boundary issues, for example, when working with two students who are in a relationship with each other or are related. Having another counsellor to work alongside was extremely helpful as was networking with other counsellors and continuous CPD. The counsellors in BACP: U&E FE mailbase has been a phenomenal support – both through the thoughtful challenges of peers but also the generosity in sharing resources and ideas for approaching novel situations.'

But do we need to have a large and diverse team of counsellors to support students successfully? Elaine, a volunteer counsellor, reflected that:

Voices

Elaine

'Although a modern college has many ethnic groups and a diverse multicultural student base, does this mean we need counsellors from different cultures? Or, as a person-centred therapist, can we use our grounding in the theory to adapt and develop psychological contact with our clients? Yes, I could, but it became easier with experience and the continuity of working in a multicultural college setting on a weekly basis. The problem being many counsellors who work in colleges are indeed students themselves with all the baggage that brings; i.e. counting hours, pressure of essay work, etc. Does that mean college counsellors are less effective?

Summary

- CPD is necessary and threefold: professional, legal and organisational.
- The complaints procedure needs to be clear and easily available to all.
- During assessment consider procedures, support, referral and confidentiality.
- There is no single accreditation scheme but several that meet different needs.
- Referrals can be internal or external and always require great care.
- The value of supervision should be recognised especially with regard to 'endings'.
- Employment status varies so there is no industry standard.

References

'CPD and the Endorsement Scheme'. Available at **http://www.bacp.co.uk/learning/CPD%20Endorsement%20Scheme/index.php** (accessed 18 January 2013).

Wheeler, S., Bowl, R. & Reeves, A. (2004) 'Assessing Risk: Confrontation or Avoidance – What is Taught on Counsellor Training Courses'. *British Journal of Guidance & Counselling*, vol. 32, no. 2, pp. 235–247.

Chapter 8
Ethical issues

'The fundamental values of counselling and psychotherapy include a commitment to:

- Respecting human rights and dignity
- Protecting the safety of clients
- Ensuring the integrity of practitioner–client relationships
- Enhancing the quality of professional knowledge and its application
- Alleviating personal distress and suffering
- Fostering a sense of self that is meaningful to the person(s) concerned
- Increasing personal effectiveness
- Enhancing the quality of relationships between people
- Appreciating the variety of human experience and culture
- Striving for the fair and adequate provision of counselling and psychotherapy services.'

BACP Ethical Framework for Good Practice in
Counselling and Psychotherapy (2010:2)

I feel that it is important to acknowledge here that the subject of ethics is so complex and far-reaching that it is impossible to cover every aspect within a single chapter. I would certainly highlight the Further Reading section at the end of this chapter if you wish to look into this area in greater depth. The areas we will be looking at in this chapter include supervision, confidentiality, safeguarding, counselling service records and legislation.

Dual roles

A counsellor is both a member of staff and has a close link with the student they are working with. This relationship can cause dilemmas such as this one that Heidi experienced:

Voices

Heidi

'There has been one incident where a very worried tutor was asking me information about a student. The tutor was clearly asking from a place of concern, but I had to field some difficult questions.'

We can see that the boundaries of confidentiality had to be clearly established here even though the tutor clearly cared. We do not want to be viewed as unhelpful or obstreperous but it is easy to see how this might happen if we are not careful.

Jane found a similar issue:

Voices

Jane

'This was a dilemma when I used to work with staff as well (no longer permitted by the college): if I heard of colleagues being bullied it would feel like I was colluding if it entirely focused on the client's experience without taking any responsibility as part of the organisation myself.'

She felt an uncomfortable sense of complicity here as again, boundaries were being tested. These are issues that would be taken to supervision and/or discussed (anonymously of course) with a line manager.

Supervision

Our main source of support and guidance is more often than not our supervisor, particularly if we are a lone worker. We know that personal supervision is necessary, not just for maintaining our professionalism, but as a valuable resource, for encouragement and motivation and for keeping us on the right track. If you are lucky enough to be working as part of a counselling team, there is the opportunity to develop peer or group supervision in addition to individual sessions.

Judy, working as a counsellor in Further Education, has a couple of points to raise in relation to her supervision. Firstly, she finds in-house group supervision a source of comfort:

Voices

Judy

'I always attend group supervision as it's a compulsory part of the role. Sometimes when I have clients I'm the only counsellor working, so I can feel quite isolated but group supervision allows me to meet up with the rest of the team. I mainly use the sessions for support but also as a type of monitoring; it puts my mind at rest when I hear similar issues being raised by my colleagues.'

Secondly, she reflects on the solace she gains from her personal supervision:

'I do find that I am affected by the impact that poor parenting has on [students], which is an ongoing theme for me in supervision. I find I can leave sessions with a feeling of deep sadness and real anger at the thoughtless and often cruel way that some parents treat their children, particularly when working with adolescents who have been raised in an environment of neglect or past abuse. I call my supervisor my "sponge of logic"; he absorbs and stabilises my feeling but keeps me focused.'

Time constraints

For many services with a well-established service and a waiting list, time limitations can be a challenge. This was highlighted as an anxiety in Chapter 4 and discussed further in Chapter 5. Restricting the number of sessions a client may attend is hardly person-centred and does not sit comfortably with many counsellors. This was explored by Caroline Hallet in her journal article 'Is there time enough? Ethical dilemmas inherent in offering time-limited work in the University'. Hallett examines the dilemmas that can arise when a counselling service is under pressure and the impact this can have upon both the counsellors and the students wishing to access counselling. She describes them being stretched to a point where counsellors are restricting sessions to four per student or even emailing students in crisis as a short-term solution until they can be offered face-to-face sessions. Hallett also identifies a key dichotomy which students can face at this vulnerable point in their lives, many having just left home for the first time and faced with having to become autonomous, self-motivating independent learners but with the requirement to meet fixed deadlines. The challenge of finding the balance between freedom and boundaries with no one else to rely on is challenging, particularly if their only learning experience has been within the tight controls of school. She includes case studies as examples to highlight the ethical decisions that need to be made to balance the safety and care of the student with the restrictions placed on the service and the general ambivalence of the university.

We can take from this that we need to open and maintain communication channels with managers keeping them aware of our challenges. In the conclusion Hallett states:

'We run the risk of responding to our own unconscious (or even conscious) desire to please the University hierarchy by colluding with the idea that all students' difficulties can be quickly and easily fixed, so that they can return to the 'real business' of academic study. To avoid the risk of colluding in this way, it becomes important to maintain dialogue between the Counselling Service and the University managers so as to alert them to our ethical concerns.'

Hallett (2012)

Confidentiality

From a geographical perspective, where should counselling be available within the institution? For most of us, this is out of our hands. It is a very lucky counselling service that can choose its location and it would be highly unlikely to achieve complete consensus regarding the options. For some, an out-of-the-way corridor or room may be most comfortable; for others, a clearly labelled department that is easy to find, or in my experience, the service that I manage has three small anonymous rooms in a very busy student services department where counselling takes place unbeknown to other students. Larger establishments tend to be housed in separate buildings or are allocated whole departments so that the team of counsellors, mental health team, reception and counselling rooms can be placed together.

In relation to funding

Voices

'There is a continuous strain around confidentiality, management can seem very suspicious of an activity taking place that they have so little knowledge of or control over. There are financial considerations – managers wanting statistics that disclose identity so that they can claim against additional learning support, and even wanting us to identify which service users are in care/care-leavers in order to claim the premium.'

We should be aware of the ethical challenges surrounding claiming for funding for students attending counselling via Additional Learning Support (**ALS**) funding. The individual names of students attending counselling might be requested to access this funding, but it is generally agreed that to provide them would be breaking confidentiality, even with their consent. There has also been discussion surrounding whether students are able to provide informed consent at this stage when they simply comply as they are wanting to access counselling so consent to attend. This is an ongoing debate with no single solution yet apparent.

In relation to other staff

Despite being employees of the educational institute, we have a rather different role to other staff, which comes with additional responsibilities. This is mainly due to the contracts and confidentiality agreements that we negotiate with our clients. There is a lot of middle ground here and challenges can often arise. For example, we may feel unsure about the level of danger a client may be in, worried about their health, their situation, their needs making maintaining our boundaries when working as part of a team an ongoing challenge. Issues can arise with regard to how the client perceives us. If they view us as counsellors and themselves as clients, the path can be smoother, however, problems can emerge if they view us as staff and themselves as students. Alternatively, how we view ourselves is of equal importance. Here is a good example of a potential conflict regarding the blurring of roles which was considered carefully and professionally:

Voices

Jane

'Students disclosing bad practice amongst colleagues has been a difficult situation. Clients sometimes moan about their teachers and I am continuously aware that I am only hearing one side of the situation and that issues about the students' own history of relationships with figures of authority etc. can play a huge part; however, occasionally I hear about a teacher's behaviour that concerns me and as a colleague, I have very much wanted to reach out to them to see what's happening. Holding clients' confidentiality can be a real challenge.'

We can see from this situation that the counsellor may worry about issues such as collusion, professionalism and whistle-blowing. As every situation is different, there are no straightforward answers, so clearly our relationship with our supervisor is vital in these situations along with our professional ethos. Being comfortable with our decisions and actions (or non-action) can be extraordinarily challenging and we should be aware that it is a strength, not a weakness, to seek support and guidance.

In relation to self-harm or risk of suicide

The challenge here is to manage the balance between on the one hand, protecting the client from themselves/others and on the other, respecting their right to autonomy. There is currently no specific legislation to cover this area so it is extremely important that our stance is clearly explained within our contracting with the client to avoid potential breaches of contract. The **BACP** Ethical Framework can provide guidance in this scenario. Bond & Mitchels (2010) provide a comprehensive list of issues to discuss with the client and supervisor:

- What has the client given me permission to do?
- Does that permission include referral?
- If I refer, what is likely to happen?
- If I do not refer, what is likely to happen?
- Do the likely consequences of non-referral include serious harm to the client or others?
- Are the likely consequences preventable?
- Is there anything I (or anyone else) can do to prevent serious harm?
- What steps would need to be taken?
- How could the client be helped to accept the proposed action?
- Does my client have the mental capacity to give explicit informed consent at this moment in time?
- If the client does not have mental capacity, then what are my professional responsibilities to the client and in the public interest?
- If the client has mental capacity, but does not consent to my proposed action (for example, referral to a GP), what is my legal situation if I go ahead and do it anyway?

We must reflect on our own abilities, limits and way of working professionally. Studies have shown that by the age of 15–16, 7 to 14 per cent of adolescents will have self-harmed once in their life (Hawton *et al*, 2002).

This situation is discussed in considerably more detail in *Challenges in Counselling: Self-harm* by Andrew Reeves (2013).

In relation to storage and sharing of notes

The method, depth and access to notes is very much dependent upon the policies of the organisation as well as the reason the notes are taken in the first place. The storage and sharing of notes is largely informed by the Data Protection Act 1998 and the Freedom of Information Act 2000. In educational counselling services, we tend to keep a record of students who attend the service, contact details, their attendance as well as notes written by counsellors at the end of each session as a record of the content. All of these can be carried out in different ways depending upon the system used by the service. Some are electronic, some paper and some a combination of the two. The security of these is extremely important to protect the details and maintain the confidentiality of who attends for counselling. It is usual for an electronic system to be password protected and encrypted to make it as secure as possible. Paper records tend to be stored in a locked cupboard in a locked room to ensure they are as safe as possible.

Some organisations request information regarding counselling practice to evidence the activities of the service which is far from straightforward; for example, if management request a list of students who attend to access funding for the counselling service. This might sound logical but there are complex ethical issues embedded within the request and subsequent solution. If we simply provide the list of names, we are breaking the confidence of our clients unless we have previously mentioned that this might be required and gained their permission. The difficulty here becomes apparent if we consider a potential client who is waiting for counselling. They are asked to provide informed consent for their name to be forwarded but they know that if they refuse, they put their counselling support in jeopardy. Is it really informed consent if there is no alternative? If we refuse to supply the names, we risk being denied funding which would put an end to our service. Unfortunately, there is no easy answer to this predicament despite it being widely experienced. What the service needs to do is substantiate their counselling activity to gain funding without compromising the confidentiality of the client base.

There are also circumstances when records are requested by outside agencies such as police, courts or healthcare services. Counselling records do not usually have to be surrendered unless requested by a judge. Even the police are not able to demand them automatically as Section 11 of the Police and Criminal Evidence Act (1984) identifies them as 'excluded material' (Bond & Mitchels, 2008:66). For further guidance I would recommend reading the work of Professor Tim Bond who writes of the legal and moral responsibilities of counsellors in a manner that is both very specific and easily accessible.

In relation to clients

To protect anonymity, it is usual for counselling services to design a code system so in documentation such as booking files and clients' records, clients are referred to by a unique code. How this is done varies from service to service but we have a very simple method. When a student first requests counselling, our administrator allocates them a code and all paperwork and online records regarding that student use that individual code. All our client codes begin with M or F, depending upon whether the client is male or female. This is followed by a two-digit number which is the year that they are attending followed by a unique number that simply indicates their place in the year. So M13-26 is a male client attending in 2013 and is the 26th male client of the year. F11-93 would be a female client who attended in 2011 and was the 93rd female client to attend that year. This means that we can easily see how many clients we have worked with at the end of each year by the final client's code. We add the male and female numbers together to give the total number of clients we worked with in any academic year. If anyone were to glance at our booking system, they would be none the wiser as to who was attending counselling. Other services use an electronic system where a code is generated by the computer system they use whilst many have developed their own system that works well for them. This recording method lessens the chance of a client's details being accidentally accessed by someone other than their counsellor and the administrator. We are also lucky enough to be able to use this code to evidence the number of students we support without having to supply their names to secure funding for the service.

Figure 8.1 Data protection and client codes

Disability

The Disability Discrimination Act 1995 (**DDA**) stipulates the rights clients have in accessing services including counselling (even if the service is provided free of charge). All clients have to be treated in an equally favourable manner with 'reasonable adjustments' being made if necessary. Section 4b is particularly relevant to counselling services. There is also the new Equality Act (2010), which brings together all of the legislation listed below into a single Act:

- Equal Pay Act 1970
- Sex Discrimination Act 1975
- Race Relations Act 1976
- Disability Discrimination Act 1995
- Employment Equality (Religion or Belief) Regulations 2003
- Employment Equality (Sexual Orientation) Regulations 2003
- Employment Equality (Age) Regulations 2006
- Equality Act 2006, Part 2
- Equality Act (Sexual Orientation) Regulations 2007.

Access, of course, is not simply physical, but services should also be considering what might be 'reasonable adjustments'. In 2004 Bernie Tuohy published an article in *BACP: U&C Journal* sharing her experiences of working with British Sign Language interpretation. There are numerous counselling services around the UK who counsel clients who are deaf (for example, **signsofhope@rcdow.org.uk**) and are able to give advice or accept referrals. In Scotland, access to deaf counsellors can be gained via the Scottish Council on Deafness (**http://www.scod.org.uk**).

Advice regarding inclusion in education is available from **http://www.skill.org.uk**.

Safeguarding

Much of this section is taken directly from our college safeguarding policy which includes definitions to illustrate our responsibilities when working with clients under 18 and protected adults. Safeguarding policies vary slightly but are, on the whole, quite similar.

Definitions

A significant number of students are under 18 years old. They are still defined as children within many aspects of the law, in particular in relation to safeguarding legislation. Safeguarding policies are designed to protect both children and protected adults. For clarity, 'protected adult' is a service-based definition and avoids labelling adults on the basis of their having a specific condition or disability. There are four categories of services, receipt of any one of which makes an individual a protected adult of which the fourth, welfare services, is most likely to apply. Welfare includes any service which provides support, assistance, advice or counselling to individuals with particular needs, meeting the following conditions. The service must be one that:

(a) is provided in the course of work to one or more persons aged 16 or over
(b) is delivered on behalf of an organisation
(c) requires training to be undertaken by the person delivering the service
(d) has a frequency and formality attached to the service, and either:
  (i) requires a contract to be agreed between the service provider and the recipient of the service prior to the service being carried out, or
  (ii) is personalised to an individual adult's needs.

Safeguarding

- Protection from abuse and neglect
- Promotion of health and development
- Ensuring safety and care
- Ensuring optimum life chances.

Child

An individual under 18 years of age.

Code of Good Practice

A Code of Good Practice highlights the steps taken to reduce everyday risk of harm (particularly accidental harm) to students and staff. It is to ensure that all forms of abuse are prevented and to support staff who work with children, young people and protected adults.

Abuse

Children and young people may be in need of protection where their basic needs are not being met, in a manner appropriate to their stage of development, and they will be at risk from avoidable acts or omissions on the part of their parent(s), sibling(s) or other relative(s), or a carer (i.e. the person(s) who, not a parent, have actual custody of a child). These categories and definitions of abuse are listed in the document 'Guidance for Education Authorities, Independent Schools, School Staff and all others working with children in an Education context in Scotland', taken from *Protecting Children – A Shared Responsibility* (1998).

Physical injury

Actual or attempted physical injury to a child, including the administration of toxic substances, where there is knowledge, or reasonable suspicion, that the injury was inflicted or knowingly not prevented.

Sexual abuse

Any child may be deemed to have been sexually abused when any person(s), by design or neglect, exploits the child, directly or indirectly, in any activity intended to lead to the sexual arousal or other forms of gratification of that person or any other person(s) including organised networks. This definition holds whether or not there has been genital contact and whether or not the child is said to have initiated, or consented to, the behaviour.

Non-organic failure to thrive

Children who significantly fail to reach normal growth and developmental milestones (for example physical growth, weight, motor, social and intellectual development), where physical and genetic reasons have been medically eliminated and a diagnosis of non-organic failure to thrive has been established.

Emotional abuse

Failure to provide for the child's basic emotional needs such as to have a severe effect on the behaviour and development of the child.

Physical neglect

This occurs when a child's essential needs are not met and this is likely to cause impairment to physical health and development. Such needs include food, clothing, cleanliness, shelter and warmth. A lack of appropriate care, including deprivation of access to healthcare, may result in persistent or severe exposure, through negligence, to circumstances which endanger the child.

Institutional abuse

When the structure of an existing organisation such as a school, learning community or sports club is used in the targeting of children and young people for abuse, this may be referred to as institutional abuse.

Responsibilities

All members of staff have a duty of care to safeguard children (individuals aged under 18 years) and protected adults from any situation where they may suffer verbal, physical, psychological abuse, bullying, harassment, ill treatment or discrimination. This policy applies to all staff, volunteers, agency workers, sub-contractors (for example cleaning and catering staff, board members and office bearers). It is the responsibility of all staff throughout the organisation to follow the safeguarding procedures and to alert the Safeguarding Officer when they believe a child or protected adult has been abused or is at risk of abuse. All complaints, allegations or suspicions must be taken seriously and reported immediately through the agreed channels.

- If you have reasonable grounds for concerns then you must listen, respond, report and record
- Stay calm
- Accept what you are being told – you do not need to decide whether or not it is true
- Listen without displaying shock or disbelief
- Reassure the student that they have done the right thing by telling you
- Show the student that you take them seriously
- Clarify anything you do not understand
- Make a note of what the student is saying as soon as possible and try and use the student's own words
- Complete appropriate Safeguarding Recording documentation
- Explain what you will do next, i.e. inform the Safeguarding Officer.

You should *not*:

- Panic
- Interrogate the student
- Guarantee confidentiality

- Act in isolation or rush into inappropriate actions
- Ask leading questions
- Make the student repeat the story unnecessarily
- Delay.

In *all* cases you must:

- Record what you have been told as soon as possible and report to the Safeguarding Officer
- You must report; do not investigate.

This is an example of the successful reporting of a safeguarding issue where the client's wants, counsellor's needs and service's policies were met in a flexible yet professional way.

Case study

During his first counselling session, Client B disclosed that he was concerned for his sister's two children as he felt they were in danger. He admitted that he knew he had to do something but was not sure what. He realised that when the counsellor explained the 'at risk' statement during his initial meeting, if he mentioned his fears he would be forced to act, as the counsellor would be in a position where they were required to pass that information on. He felt this would be helpful. As soon as he disclosed his suspicions the counsellor stopped the counselling session and explained that they would need to act on this information. Client B stated that his greatest fear was losing track of the information rather like in the game of Chinese Whispers. The counsellor felt that as she had no direct evidence and was working on hearsay, in this case it was more appropriate to contact the Social Work Family Protection Unit rather than the police. Client B agreed. A telephone was brought into the counselling room and the counsellor dialled the number for the social work department. When she was transferred to the appropriate member of staff in the Family Protection Unit, she passed the telephone to Client B and left the room. Client B spoke in private to the Social Worker for some time, left the counselling room, thanked the counsellor and made another counselling appointment for the following week. The counsellor then re-dialled the Family Protection social worker to check that they had indeed spoken to Client B which was confirmed (although no discussion regarding content took place so no confidentiality agreement was broken).

- The counsellor felt comfortable with the process as she felt she had adhered to the Service Safeguarding Policy but in a manner that respected her client's wishes.
- The client was happy as he had been supported in dealing with the situation in a manner that kept him in control of the information.
- The service manager was happy with the process as she felt it had been handled sensitively and professionally.

Three months after completing counselling, the Service received an email from Client B thanking them for their respectful handling of the situation and confirming that all was well; the children were safe and at home and at no further risk.

Relevant legislation and guidelines

England/UK

- Access to Health Records 1990.
- Access to Medical Reports 1988.
- Human Rights Act 1998.
- The Sexual Offences Act 2003.
- The Children Act (1989) and (2004).
- Safeguarding Vulnerable Groups Act 2006.
- The Rehabilitation of Offenders Act 1974.
- The Data Protection Act 1998.
- Education Act 2002.
- Freedom of Information Act 2000.
- United Nations convention on the Rights of the Child, ratified by the UK Government in 1991.

Northern Ireland

The Children (Northern Ireland) Order 1995.

Wales

- Safeguarding children: working together under the Children Act 2004 (Welsh Assembly Government, 2006).

Scotland

- Additional Support for Learning (Scotland) Act 2004 (amended 2009).
- 'It's everyone's job to make sure I'm alright'. Scottish Executive, November 2002.
- 'Legislation outlines in Annex C of Protecting Children and Young People: Framework for Standards'. Scottish Executive, March 2004.
- *Protecting Children – A Shared Responsibility – Guidance on Inter-Agency Co-operation*. Scottish Office, 1998.
- The Children (Scotland) Act 1995.
- The Protection of Children (Scotland) Act 2003.
- Part V, The Police (Scotland) Act (1997).
- The Protection of Vulnerable Groups (PVG) (Scotland) Act 2007.
- 'Protecting Children and Young People: The Charter'. Scottish Executive, March 2004.
- The Age of Legal Capacity (Scotland) Act 1991.
- National Guidance for Child Protection in Scotland. The Scottish Government, 2010.

Further reading

Information and relevant, up-to-date publications are available at **http://www.education.gov.uk.**

Bond, T. & Mitchels, B. (2010) 'Breaches in Confidentiality' *(G2 Information Sheet)*. Lutterworth: BACP.

Bowman, B. & Payne, J. (2011) 'A Profile of Students Receiving Counselling Services at a University in Post-apartheid South Africa'. *Journal of Child & Adolescent Mental Health*, Vol. 23, No. 2, pp. 143–153.

Burchell, S. (2008) 'Counselling Asylum Seekers and Refugees'. *G8 Information Sheet*. Lutterworth: BACP.

Coldridge, L. (2010) 'Making Notes and Records of Counselling and Psychotherapy Sessions'. *P12 Information Sheet*. Lutterworth: BACP.

Dale, H. (2010) 'Am I Fit to Practise as a Counsellor?' *P9 Information Sheet*. Lutterworth: BACP.

Gabriel, L. & Casemore, R. (2010) 'Guidance for Ethical Decision Making: A Suggested Model for Practitioners'. *P4 Information Sheet*. Lutterworth: BACP.

Hallett, C. (2012) 'Is there time enough? Ethical dilemmas inherent in offering time-limited work in the University'. *British Journal of Psychotherapy*, vol. 28, no. 2

Hawton, K., Rodham, K., Evans, E. & Weatherall, R. (2002) 'Deliberate Self-harm in Adolescents: Self Report Survey in Schools in England'. *British Medical Journal*, 325: 1207–1211.

Her Majesty's Government/Department of Health (2012) 'Preventing Suicide in England: A Cross-government Outcomes Strategy to Save Lives'. London: Department of Health.

Jones, M. (2012) 'Surrendering Counselling Notes to the Police of Courts'. *AUCC Journal*. September 2012, p.27.

Peden, A. (2010) 'Recognising and Acting Upon Child Sexual Abuse'. *G18 Information Sheet*. Lutterworth: BACP.

Reeves, A. & Seber, P. (2010) 'Working with the Suicidal Client'. *P7 Information Sheet*. Lutterworth: BACP.

Robson, D. & Robson, M. (2000) 'Ethical issues in Internet Counselling'. *Counselling Psychology Quarterly*, vol. 13, no. 3, pp. 249–257.

Setiawan, J.L. (2006) 'Willingness to Seek Counselling, and Factors that Facilitate and Inhibit the Seeking of Counselling in Indonesian Undergraduate Students'. *British Journal of Guidance & Counselling*, vol. 34, no. 3, pp. 403–419.

Reference

Bond, T. & Mitchels, B. (2010) 'Breaches in Confidentiality'. *G2 Information Sheet*. Lutterworth: BACP.

Chapter 9
Research

There are lots of books available that explain how to conduct research. There are also thousands of papers available on research that has already been conducted over the years in relation to university and college counselling services. In this chapter, I have sourced a small number of papers; some research-based and some reviewing research. I have purposely chosen a range that touches on the wide spectrum of areas to consider, including different settings and different areas of interest, for example, students' mental wellbeing, retention, stress, and students' different countries. You will notice that some of the articles were published some time ago but remain relevant as we consider what can be learned from their work and how we integrate any findings into our practice. If this is an area of particular interest, I would recommend reading *A Systematic Scoping Review of the Research on Counselling in Higher and Further Education*, commissioned by **BACP** in 2006, which briefly discusses relevance and findings. Not surprisingly, when Glynis Breakwell evaluated student counselling literature between 1962 and 1986, she noted that the majority of research was small-scale and took place within institutions' own services, which I suspect is still the case today.

'Dropping out of University: A Statistical Analysis of the Probability of Withdrawal for UK University Students' (Smith & Naylor, 2001)

Although the statistical content of this paper is from a number of years ago, Smith and Naylor found evidence to support that a student's ability to complete their course is influenced by their prior academic preparedness and also their social integration (which interestingly is also identified in Gallacher *et al*'s 2000 study below). There is also discussion of students from a four-year course being more likely to drop out than those on a three-year course in addition to the drop-out rate of first-year students.

What can we learn from this?

This study found that 'the probability of dropping out of university is influenced significantly by pre-university education, personal attributes, the degree subject and characteristics of the department and university'. Whether we agree with it or not, our institutions see our role as supporting students' mental wellbeing and thus enabling them to succeed on their course. We therefore need to be aware of the context of the student's world and develop a sense of their history and experiences if we are to support them successfully. This holistic approach echoes the findings in the following study.

'Evaluating the Impact of Receiving University-based Counselling Services on Student Retention' (Wilson *et al*, 1997)

Wilson *et al* studied the academic outcomes of 562 students who had attended counselling two years previously. They state that 'The results of the present study suggest that receiving psychological counselling can have an impact on a student's likelihood of succeeding in college. Counselled students enjoyed a 14 per cent retention advantage over their non-counselled counterparts.'

What can we learn from this?

Despite this being a study conducted within a single university, it is interesting to read that, 'Perhaps counselling helps certain students to negotiate critical periods in their lives when they are especially vulnerable to dropping out.' They also suggest that attending counselling might not only support students during a crisis, but that 'Others may acquire new social skills that help them to be more successful at meeting their needs and thereby to feel more integrated into the social world of the university.'

'Silently Stressed: A Survey into Student Mental Wellbeing' (NUS, 2010)

In the NUS Scotland report 'Silently Stressed', there is some very helpful data. For example, following a survey of over 1,800 students in 2011 it was found that:

- 75 per cent of student mental services reported increased demand from last year
- 40 per cent of university services reported they could not meet this increased demand
- 80 per cent of respondents stated that they felt the stigma surrounding the issue of mental ill-health would act as a barrier in coming forward for help
- 29 per cent of students would feel able to approach their academic mentor if they were experiencing mental health problems
- 17.3 per cent would feel able to approach support services
- 11.3 per cent would feel able to approach their student association
- 6.8 per cent would feel able to approach external organisations.

In the follow-up report 'Breaking the Silence', published in 2011, the findings were analysed. An area that I have found of particular interest is where students indicated where they were most likely to access mental health support, 55.8 per cent stated that they would approach their family first, 54.9 per cent their friends, 37.5 per cent would contact their GP, 29.4 per cent their academic mentor and 17.3 per cent the institution's counselling services; 11.3 per cent would approach the students' association with 6.8 per cent preferring external organisations. The survey clearly established that, in Scotland at least, the greatest barrier for a student wanting to ask for support (at 82.9 per cent) would be the perceived stigma and embarrassment involved. I found this report to be detailed, very easy to read and freely available online, making it a very useful resource.

Figure 9.1 Promoting student mental health

What can we learn from this?

There are several recommendations made throughout, with a focus on general growth in this area:

'Universities and colleges need to invest to ensure they have sufficient support services to provide help for students with mental ill-health. This is particularly important in the college sector, where many institutions reported that they provided no specific help for mental ill-health among their students.'

NUS (2010)

Another recommendation is that 'Universities and colleges should consider providing mental health related training for lecturing staff, enabling them to provide immediate support and referral if and when required'; along with 'Universities and colleges must work with their respective students' associations to consider ways in which barriers to asking for support may be removed'.

'Education for All? Further Education, Social Inclusion and Widening Access' (Gallacher *et al*, 2000) and 'Learning careers and the social space: exploring the fragile identities of adult returners in the new further education' (Gallacher *et al*, 2002)

I found these two papers of great interest in considering and understanding adult learners in **FE** from a social perspective. The 2000 study includes interviews with a range of students (adult returners, young people and adults with learning difficulties) highlighting the non-traditional learners' difficulties and challenges. Although the role of counselling is not discussed, there is much focus on support and relationships within the learning environment. The conclusions identify a range of barriers that our students can face including financial, social exclusion, childcare responsibilities, attitudes and structural constraints.

What we can learn from this?

Firstly, supportive networks and strong relationships are clearly emphasised as being a key factor in whether the students feel they are able to achieve or not. Secondly, the student's own self-image is a crucial indicator as to whether they will stay the length of the course; if a student has confidence in their abilities and a sense of purpose and social connectedness, they are more likely to pass. As counsellors, we might expect students to present with issues surrounding hardship and unemployment: students may have had low levels of achievement in school and a negative attitude towards schooling, financial constraints, childcare responsibilities, travel difficulties and age-related challenges: 'Many adults perceived their age an important barrier to participation. They view **FE** as being for younger students and not for them.'

'Retention and Wastage in FE and HE' (Hall, 2001)

I have included this review of research literature as there are elements of the general statements made in it which I feel we, as counsellors, often forget. For example, 'Institutions are unlikely to eliminate drop-out', and 'Reasons for student drop-out are usually multiple and complex', along with 'Drop-out rates are higher in further education than in higher education, but no overall figures are available'.

I mention these three in particular, as my experience of supporting students is that we can often be very critical of ourselves and if one of our clients leaves their course, we can question our own role in their decision, in a manner that goes beyond professional reflection and can touch on regret or dissatisfaction of our own way of working. It is clearly mentioned that 'colleges and universities can help through pre-course guidance, induction programmes, in-course monitoring and counselling for "at-risk" students'. So there is recognition that counselling has a part to play in supporting students (although it is not completely clear in what context counselling is meant).

What can we learn from this?

By remembering that there will always be students who leave their course; we cannot be held personally responsible for our clients deciding the barriers to their studying are greater than their coping strategies and by taking solace from the majority of our clients overcoming their difficulties to continuing on their course.

'Counsellors' Perceptions of Adolescence' (Tatar, 2001)

At first glance this research may look out of place in a book focusing on adults, but despite being set in Israeli schools and being from 2001, I have chosen to include this study because the identification of five types of adolescents can be helpful when working with younger clients. These types are categorised as:

- **The drive-orientated adolescent**, perceived as being controlled by their hormones and finds difficulty in overcoming impulses, many of which are physical.
- **The intellectually-oriented adolescent**, viewed as complex due to their ability for abstract thought, focus on success, intelligence and mental abilities. They can find it difficult to connect with other students of the same age if they deem them to be less able.
- **The group-orientated adolescent**, mainly influenced by their peer group and desperately want to fit in. What others think of them is of huge importance and accessing counselling would only be acceptable if a counsellor is 'popular and accepted by the group as a legitimate source of assistance'.
- **The community-oriented adolescent**, who dedicates much of their time to community-based activities and volunteering. Because of this they may be perceived as more mature than their peers. They can invest more time into their extracurricular activities than their school work but this additional work is appreciated and valued by adults.
- **The isolated adolescent** is a lonely and depressed young person. Counsellors expressed concerns with regard to their success and tried a range of strategies when working with these adolescents.

What can we learn from this?

'The counsellors' interviews indicated a need for the development and adaptation of various counselling strategies for dealing with the different types of adolescents.' The conclusions also include acknowledgment of some difficulties counsellors experienced when working with adolescents such as:

i) establishing the initial rapport
ii) fully understanding what the adolescents expect from the counsellor
iii) reducing the stigma according to which counsellors 'only deal with problematic kids'
iv) continuing counselling after the first (and usually only) counselling session
v) going beyond prejudicial perceptions of the 'typical' adolescent (mainly the drive-oriented type)
vi) finding the professional means by which to convince adolescents that school counsellors are their best advocates and can be trusted.

This applies equally to the FE sector, where it is not uncommon for us to be working therapeutically with 15- and 16-year-olds. I find it helpful to be reminded that adolescents often think, feel and act in very different ways to mature adults.

'Evaluating the Effectiveness of Short-term Treatment at a University Counseling Center' (Vonk & Thyer, 1999)

This is an American study that aimed to measure the efficacy of undetermined short-term counselling. It was based on 55 participants; clients who attended more than four but fewer than twenty counselling sessions, and the Symptom CheckList-90-Revised (**SCL-90-R**) was used as an outcome measure. The findings were that short-term counselling is effective. These results reinforce the already upheld opinion that short-term counselling is no less effective than long-term counselling for clients with a higher degree of psychopathology.

What can we learn from this?

Despite being a small study, the article does highlight the value of making counselling available for students, even if we are restricted in the number of sessions we are able to offer. Any sessions are better than no sessions even with a client who is experiencing a greater level of disturbance. Whilst reading this, we might also bear in mind the findings of Turner *et al* who, in 1996, found that there was no difference in student satisfaction whether they received 30- or 50-minute counselling sessions.

'Student Mental Health: How can Psychiatrists Better Support the Work of University Medical Centres and University Counselling Services?' (Waller *et al*, 2005)

This study recognises the role counselling support has in the retention and success of student outcomes and the significant data there is available to support this but found a dearth of similar literature on psychiatric support. This paper acknowledges the increase in mental health issues presenting in university counselling services and considers the addition of psychiatric help being available in addition to counselling. They establish arguments for and against having a dedicated psychiatric team based in universities.

What can we learn from this?

There is a lot of interesting information contained in this paper and it is very specific to the University of Leeds. Again there are a number of aspects that can be extrapolated to make it more universal. Firstly we can note that 'Liaison between the different services can be of advantage to individual students', which is not too surprising. Secondly, 'Boundaries would also be necessary so students didn't come to see the Student Counselling Centre as a quasi-medical service', and finally, 'It is suggested that it is necessary to provide dedicated psychiatric input well before this stage if drop-out from university is to be prevented'. We can't simply be aware of increased incidents of mental illness: we need to make strides in developing support mechanisms that are sufficiently robust to supplement the counselling teams.

'Degrees of Disturbance: The New Agenda. The Impact of Increasing Levels of Psychological Disturbance Amongst Students in Higher Education' (Rana et al, 1999)

Despite this report being published in 1999, its content is still regularly cited. It was written by a working group, consisting of managers of university counselling services when it was noticed that there was an increase in students with severe psychological problems presenting to university counselling services. This was also at a time when the government initiative to increase access to higher education was beginning.

What can we learn from this?

The paper was mainly intended to promote discussion, but a number of recommendations are made. They confirm a need to 'develop and implement cultures, structures and policies to promote mental wellbeing for both students and staff' and list recommendations for counselling services:

'We would suggest that counselling services should build on existing good practice to make the following contributions:

- supporting students who are distressed or disturbed

- supporting those who are concerned about the mental health of such students

- liaising with other mental health professionals in the community and, where appropriate, working with medical, psychiatric and nursing staff attached to their institutions and in local hospitals

- assisting in the formulation and development of institutional policies and providing feedback to institutions about the implementation of such policies

- fostering better communication between counselling services and statutory and voluntary agencies in order that their respective roles and boundaries can be clarified to foster more effective co-operation wherever possible

- working in partnership with other areas of the institution in order to help students make the most of their learning opportunities

- offering training to other staff to help raise the general level of personal tutorial support within institutions, for example, workshops, and link with institutional teaching programmes for staff.'

'The Impact of Counselling in Further and Higher Education: Briefing on Recent Research Findings' (BACP, 2012)

Patti Wallace conducted this national research using questionnaires that were completed by students who had received in-house counselling during their studies. Responses were received from more than 5,500 students from 65 different universities and colleges throughout the UK so the findings are fairly representative.

'Retention: 54% of all student respondents indicated that counselling was either "an important factor" or "the most significant factor",

Achievement: 50.6% of all student respondents indicated that counselling was either "an important factor" or "the most significant factor",

Student experience: 55.9% of all students indicated that counselling was either "an important factor" or "the most significant factor",

Employability: 59.9% of all students indicated that counselling was either "an important factor" or "the most significant factor".

What can we learn from this?

The results support the efficacy of counselling intervention. Wallace's conclusions state that:

'based on the quantitative findings, we can conclude that over 75% of students who completed counselling within the 2011/12 academic year at the 65 institutions involved in the research found that counselling:

- helped them stay at university or college

- improved their academic achievement

- improved their overall experience of being a student

- helped them develop employability skills.'

Stigma

There have been several studies on the impact that stigma surrounding attending counselling can have on students (Vogel et al, 2007; Hobson, 2008; Beach, 2009), so this is yet another area to be examining although, many of the findings identify a wider, more general attitudinal bias within the culture of society, rather than being contained within the student population.

Micro-research

Within our college (in line with Breakwell's findings in 1987), we measure the counselling service statistics on an annual basis, in line with the academic year (August to June). This is carried out anonymously with no students' personal details included. We measure the number of sessions delivered each year, the number of students who attend, the gender of these students, the presenting issues, **DNAs** and **CNAs**. For example, the number of appointments made a month can be compared to previous years to highlight any peaks and troughs. We can see here that

November, March and May were the busiest months in 2011–12, which just happens to be the end of the three terms when most assessments take place. This information is used in several ways:

- to feed back to management to illustrate that there is an ongoing need for the service
- to help us learn more about our students and how we can support them
- to identify any themes that emerge, such as students on a course experiencing similar issues
- to inform our future planning so our counselling service remains helpful, for example, employing counsellors who speak more than one language
- to help with marketing and raising awareness
- to adhere to professional guidelines.

If conducting research is of interest for you, more information on establishing facts and truths in counselling practice can be found in *Challenges in Counselling: Research* by Jim Carmichael (Hodder Education, 2013).

Further reading

Carmichael, J. (2013) *Challenges in Counselling: Research*. London: Hodder Education.

References

BACP (2012) *The Impact of Counselling in Further and Higher Education: Briefing on Recent Research Findings*. Lutterworth: BACP.

Beach, E. (2009) 'Perspectives on the Academy: Educational Counselling and Stigma'. *Annual Review of Education, Communication and Life Sciences*, vol. 6, pp. 18–34. Available at **http://research.ncl.ac.uk/ARECLS/** (accessed 16 October 2012).

Breakwell, G. (1987) 'The evaluation of student counselling: A review of the literature 1962–86'. *British Journal of Guidance and Counselling*, vol. 15, no. 2, pp. 131–9.

Gallacher, J., Crossan, B., Leahy, J., Merrill, B. & Field, J. (2000) *Education for All? Further Education, Social Inclusion and Widening Access*. Available at **http://www.crll.org.uk/knowledge-exchange/publications/researchreports/** (accessed 16 October 2012).

Gallacher, J., Crossan, B., Field J. & Merrill, B. (2002) 'Learning careers and the social space: exploring the fragile identities of adult returners in the new further education'. *International Journal of Lifelong Education*, vol. 21, no. 6, pp. 493–509.

Hall, J.C. (2001) *Retention and Wastage in FE and HE.* University of Ulster: SCRE.

Hobson, H.L. (2008) *The Effect of Mental Health Education on Reducing Stigma and Increasing Positive Attitudes Toward Seeking Therapy.* Unpublished MA Thesis. Available at **http://humboldt-dspace.calstate. edu/handle/2148/371** (accessed 18 January 2013).

NUS (2010). 'Silently Stressed: A Survey into Student Mental Wellbeing'. Available at **http://www.nus.org.uk/en/Campaigns/Campaigns-in-Scotland/Student-Mental-Health/Silently-Stressed/** (accessed October 2012).

NUS (2011) 'Breaking the Silence: The Follow up Report to Silently Stressed'. Available at **http://www.nus.org.uk/Documents/ NUS%20Scotland/Breaking%20The%20Silence.pdf** (accessed October 2012).

Rana, R., Smith, E, & Walkling, J. (1999) *Degrees of Disturbance: The New Agenda: The Impact of Increasing Levels of Psychological Disturbance Amongst Students in Higher Education.* Rugby: British Association of Counselling.

Smith, J.P. & Naylor, R.A. (2001) 'Dropping out of University: A Statistical Analysis of the Probability of Withdrawal for UK University Students'. *Journal of the Royal Statistical Society*, vol. 164, no. 2, pp. 389–405.

Tatar, M. (2001) 'Counsellors' perceptions of adolescence'. *British Journal of Guidance & Counselling*, vol. 29, no. 2, pp. 213–231.

Turner P.R., Valtierra, M., Talken, T.R., Miller, V.I. & DeAnda, J. (1996) 'Effect of Session Length on Treatment Outcome for College Students in Brief Therapy'. *Journal of Counseling Psychology*, 43:228–232.

Vogel, D.L., Wade, N.G. & Hackler, A.H. (2007) 'Perceived Public Stigma and the Willingness to Seek Counseling: The Mediating Roles of Self-Stigma and Attitudes Toward Counseling'. *Journal of Counselling Psychology*, vol. 54, no. 1, pp. 40–50.

Vonk, M.E. & Thyer, B.A. (1999) 'Evaluating the Effectiveness of Short-term Treatment at a University Counseling Center'. *Journal of Clinical Psychology*, vol. 55, no. 9, pp. 1095–1106.

Waller, R., Mahmood, T., Gandi, R., Delves, S., Humphrys, N. & Smith, D. (2005) 'Student Mental Health: How can Psychiatrists Better Support the Work of University Medical Centres and University Counselling Services?' *British Journal of Guidance and Counselling*, vol. 33, no. 1, pp. 117–128.

Wilson, S.B., Mason, T.W. & Ewing, M.J.M. (1997) 'Evaluating the Impact of Receiving University-based Counseling Services on Student Retention'. *Journal of Counseling and Psychology*, vol. 44, no. 3, pp. 316–320.

List of abbreviations

Figure 10.1

ALS
Additional Learning Support.

AMOSSHE
Association of Managers of Student Services in Higher Education. They support their members, focus on the student experience and influence policymaking.

AUCC
Association for University and College Counselling, now called BACP: U&E. AUCC is a division of **BACP**. They provide information, guidance and discussion forums for their members.

BACP
British Association for Counselling and Psychotherapy. BACP is the UK's largest professional counselling accrediting body.

BAHSHE
British Association of Healthcare Services for Students in Higher Education.

CBT
Cognitive behavioural therapy. A form of counselling that challenges cognitive distortions.

CLC
Community learning centre. A centre some distance from an educational institution specifically to engage hard-to-reach students who would otherwise not be able to study.

CMHT
Community mental health team. Comprises a range of mental health professionals.

CNA
Could not attend. Used when clients miss an appointment but contact the service beforehand to inform them. See also **DNA**.

CORE-OM
Clinical Outcomes in Routine Evaluation. This is a generic psychological measurement tool that is widely used to monitor client progress. It consists of 34 questions that cover four core areas of wellbeing, symptoms, functioning and risk. There is a shorter version, CORE-10.

COSCA
Confederation of Scottish Counselling Agencies.

CPCAB
Counselling and Psychotherapy Central Awarding Body.

CPD
Continuing professional development. The means by which people maintain their knowledge and skills relating to their professional lives.

CT
Cognitive therapy.

CVCP
Committee of Vice-Chancellors and Principals (now **Universities UK**).

DDA
Disability Discrimination Act (1995). Schedule 4B relates to educational institutions.

DNA
Did not attend. A client who misses a counselling session without notifying the service of their absence.

DSA
Disabled Students' Allowance.

EAP
Employee Assistance Programme. This is where an external counselling service is used.

FE
Further Education. The term does not simply refer to a college but to a level of learning. FE courses tend to be at a non-advanced or basic introductory level and are a bridge between qualifications delivered within schools and higher level courses. FE courses can occasionally be delivered in universities.

HE
Higher Education. We often talk of HE in respect of universities but HE (like **FE**) refers to the level of a course. HE courses are delivered in both colleges and universities. HE refers to courses above **FHEQ** level 4f or **SCQF** level 7.

HEFCE
Higher Education Funding Council for England.

HEFCW
Higher Education Funding Council for Wales.

HERO
Higher Education Research Opportunities.

HESA
Higher Education Statistics Agency.

HMIE
Her Majesty's Inspector of Education, the Scottish equivalent of **Ofsted**. They carry out independent inspections of tertiary education providers such as colleges as well as schools and provide publicly available reports on their findings.

HNC
Higher National Certificate. HNC courses are made up of a collection of units worth 12 credits in the same way that **National Certificate (NC)** courses are. However, despite being mainly delivered within colleges they are **HE** level and are the equivalent of the first year of a degree (**FHEQ** level 4 or **SCQF** level 7), so many **HNC**s articulate into the second year of a degree.

HND
Higher National Diploma. HND courses are the equivalent of the second year of a degree (**FHEQ** level 5 or **SCQF** level 8). They are often the next step on from an HNC and consist of 15 units.

HUCS
Heads of University Counselling Services (a special interest group of **BACP: U&E**).

IAPT
Improving Access to Psychological Therapies.

LSA
Learning and Skills Agency, formerly Further Education Development Agency (FEDA).

MMT
Multi-modal therapy.

MWBHE
Universities UK/Guild HE Working Group for the Promotion of Mental Well-Being in Higher Education.

NAMSS
National Association Medical Staff Services. Support for Student Services Managers in Colleges.

NC or NQ
National Certificate or National Qualification. NC or NQ courses are non-advanced courses that consist of a collection of units (usually 12–15) that make up the group award.

NUS
National Union of Students. Their website is an informative and easily accessible source of information on mental health and wellbeing for students.

Ofsted
Office for Standards in Education, Children's Services and Skills. Ofsted is an independent body which inspects and regulates educational establishments such as colleges and schools and reports to Parliament.

ONC
Ordinary National Certificate.

PCT
Person-centered therapy.

QAA
Quality Assurance Agency for Higher Education.

REBT
Rational emotive behavioural theory.

SCL-90-R
Stands for Symptom CheckList-90-Revised. It is a relatively brief psychological measurement tool that is widely used to measure psychological distress in clinical practice and research. It consists of 90 items and takes 12–15 minutes to administer.

SCOP
Standing Conference of Principals.

SCQF
Scottish Credit Qualifications Framework. Qualifications Framework is the equivalent of the **FHEQ** (Framework for Higher Education Qualifications). The SCQF provides a structure to compare the level of courses. It allows for parallels and equivalents to be made which is necessary when applying for Accredited Prior Learning (APL). Further information can be accessed at **http://www.scqf.org.uk**.

SENDA
Special Educational Needs and Disability Act 2001.

SFA
Skills Funding Agency.

SFC
Scottish Funding Council.

SHEFC
Scottish Higher Education Funding Council.

SLT
Social learning theory.

TA
Transactional analysis.

UMHAN
University Mental Health Advisors Network.

Universities UK
The representative organisation for UK Universities. The website includes detailed information on **HE** throughout the UK.

VLE
Virtual Learning Environment. A VLE is a website that contains learning materials, which does not only provide access to teaching materials but also allows students to submit assessments remotely. There are usually discussion forums included as an additional form of communication between students and tutors. This is an expanding method of delivering teaching materials and is of particular importance in distance learning and for students who are geographically distanced from their education centre. Examples of VLEs include Blackboard and Moodle.

YPLA
Young People's Learning Agency.

Appendix

Recognition and comparison of courses in different parts of the UK

We have discussed how courses, awards and qualifications can be compared in relation to their level. This is a useful tool when we come to consider Accredited Prior Learning (APL), Recognition of Prior Learning (RPL), Accreditation of Prior Experiential Learning (APEL) or Recognition of Prior Experiential Learning (RPEL).

This table on the following page may be of use when reflecting upon our own career development or to gain an understanding of our students.

Main stages of education/employment	Framework for higher education qualifications in England, Wales and Northern Ireland www.qaa.ac.uk/assuringstandardsandquality/qualifications		Qualifications and Credit Framework/National Qualifications Framework for England and Northern Ireland www.ofqual.gov.uk www.ccea.org.uk		Credit and Qualifications Framework for Wales www.cqfw.net		National Framework of Qualifications for Ireland www.nfq.ie		The Scottish Credit and Qualifications Framework www.scqf.org.uk	
	Level		Level		Level		Level		Level	
Professional or postgraduate education, research or employment	8	Doctoral Degrees	8	Vocational Qualifications Level 8	8	Doctoral Degrees	10	Doctoral Degree, Higher Doctorate	12	Professional Development Awards, Doctoral Degrees
Higher education / Advanced skills training	7	Master's Degrees, Integrated Master's Degrees, Postgraduate Diplomas, Postgraduate Certificate in Education (PGCE), Postgraduate Certificates	7	Fellowships, NVQ Level 5, Vocational Qualifications Level 7	7	Master's Degrees, Integrated Master's Degrees, Postgraduate Diplomas, Postgraduate Certificate in Education (PGCE), Postgraduate Certificates	9	Master's Degree, Post-graduate Diploma	11	SVQ Level 5, Professional Development Awards, Postgraduate Diplomas, Master's Degrees, Integrated Master's Degrees, Postgraduate Certificates
									10	Bachelor's Degrees with Honours, Professional Development Awards, Graduate Diplomas, Graduate Certificates

Category	Level		Level		Level		Level		Level	
	6	Bachelor's Degrees with Honours, Bachelor's Degrees, Professional Graduate Certificate in Education (PGCE), Graduate Diplomas, Graduate Certificates	6	Vocational Qualifications Level 6	6	Bachelor's Degrees with Honours, Bachelor's Degrees, Professional Graduate Certificate in Education (PGCE), Graduate Diplomas, Graduate Certificates	8	Honours Bachelor Degree, Higher Diploma	9	Bachelor's/ Ordinary Degrees, Professional Development Awards, SVQ Level 4, Graduate Diplomas, Graduate Certificates
Entry to professional graduate employment	5	Foundation Degrees, Diplomas of Higher Education (DipHE), Higher National Diplomas (HND)	5	NVQ Level 4, Higher National Diplomas (HND), Vocational Qualifications Level 5	5	Foundation Degrees, Diplomas of Higher Education (DipHE), Higher National Diplomas (HND)	7	Ordinary Bachelor Degree	8	Higher National Diplomas, SVQ Level 4, Professional Development Awards, Diplomas of Higher Education (DipHE)
Specialised education and training	4	Higher National Certificates (HNC), Certificates of Higher Education (CertHE)	4	Vocational Qualifications Level 4, Higher National Certificates (HNC)	4	Higher National Certificates (HNC), Certificates of Higher Education (CertHE), NVQ level 4, Essential Skills Wales (ESW), Wider Key Skills (WKS), Higher Apprenticeship Framework	6	Advanced Certificate, Higher Certificate	7	Professional Development Awards, Higher National Certificates, Certificates of Higher Education (CertHE), SVQ Level 3, Scottish Baccalaureate, Advanced Highers

Continued

Main stages of education/ employment	Framework for higher education qualifications in England, Wales and Northern Ireland www.qaa.ac.uk/ assuringstandard-sandquality/ qualifications	Qualifications and Credit Framework/ National Qualifications Framework for England and Northern Ireland www.ofqual.go v.uk www.ccea.org.uk	Credit and Qualifications Framework for Wales www.cqfw.net	National Framework of Qualifications for Ireland www.nfq.ie	The Scottish Credit and Qualifications Framework www.scqf.org.uk
Qualified/ Skilled worker Entry to higher education Completion of secondary education		3 NVQ Level 3, Vocational Qualifications Level 3, GCE AS and A Level, Advanced Diplomas (England)	3 NVQ Level 3, ESW, WKS, Vocational Qualifications Level 3, GCE AS and A Level, Welsh Baccalaureate Qualification Advanced, Apprenticeships Framework	5 Level 5 Certificate, Leaving Certificate	6 Highers, SVQ Level 3, Professional Development Awards, National Progression Awards, National Certificates
Progression to skilled employment Continuation of secondary education		2 NVQ Level 2, Vocational Qualifications Level 2, GCSEs at grade A*–C, ESOL skills for life, Higher Diplomas (England), functional skills Level 2 (England) (English, mathematics & ICT), Essential Skills Qualifications (NI)	2 NVQ Level 2, Vocational Qualifications Level 2, Welsh Baccalaureate Qualification Intermediate, GCSEs grade A*–C, ESW, WKS, Foundation Apprenticeship Framework	4 Level 4 Certificate, Leaving Certificate	5 Intermediate 2, Credit Standard Grade, SVQ Level 2, National Progression Awards, National Certificates

Secondary education. Initial entry into employment or further education	1	NVQ Level 1, Vocational Qualifications Level 1, GCSEs at grade D–G, ESOL skills for life, Foundation Diplomas (England), Functional Skills Level 1 (England) (English, mathematics & ICT), Essential Skills Qualifications (NI)	1	NVQ Level 1, ESW, WKS, Vocational Qualifications Level 1, GCSEs at grade D–G, Welsh Baccalaureate Qualification Foundation	3	Level 3 Certificate, Junior Certificate	4	Intermediate 1, General Standard Grade, SVQ Level 1, National Progression Awards, National Certificates
	Entry Level	Entry Level Certificates (sub levels 1–3), ESOL skills for life, Functional Skills Entry Level (England) (English, mathematics & ICT), Essential Skills Qualifications (NI)	Entry Level	Entry Level Qualifications, ESW	2	Level 2 Certificate	3	Access 3, Foundation Standard Grades, National Progression Awards, National Certificates
					1	Level 2 Certificate	2	Access 2, National Progression Awards, National Certificates
							1	Access 1

Figure 10.2 Table from 'Qualification can cross boundaries', QAA, reproduced with the permission of QAA. Leaflet available from www.qaa.ac.uk/Publications/InformationAndGuidance/Pages/qualifications-can-cross-boundaries.aspx

Index

abuse 85, 112–13
academic stress, meaning 85
academic year, nature/ phases of
    related counselling issues 21–2, 54, 130
accreditation 93–4
addictive behaviour 85
Additional Learning Support 105
Adler, A. 28, 36
adolescents
    counsellors' understanding of 124–5
    types of 125
adult learners
    learning, attitudes to 10–11, 79–81, 123
    particular challenges 22, 54, 123
advertising counselling services 82, 94–5
age, of students see also safeguarding
    influence on counselling 8, 10, 80, 123
Ainsworth, M. 36
anger issues 85
anxiety 85
Association for University and College
       Counselling (AUCC) 93
associative learning 31
attachment theory 36–7
autonomy issues 21, 107
Bandura, A. 31–2
Barnes, B. 68
Beck, A. 32–3
behaviour modification 31
behavioural theories 30
    classical and operant conditioning 31
    social learning theory (SLT) 31–2
Berne, E. 28
boundaries, cultural differences in attitudes
       to 66
Bowlby, J. 36–7
Breakwell, G. 119
British Association for Counselling and
       Psychotherapy (BACP)
    accreditation 93
    aims 3
    continual professional development 91
    ethical framework 101, 107
    guidance notes 6–7, 11
    study of impact of counselling in FE/ HE
       128–9
British Psychology Society (BPS) 93

budgeting
    constraints and strategies 59–60
    institutional conflicts of interest 48–9
burn-out 51–2
challenges
    adolescents, understanding and dealing
       with 124–5
    cessation of studies and continuity of
       counselling 52, 71, 83
    combined student/ staff services 17,
       47–8, 62–4
    confidentiality 48, 55–6, 66, 69, 102, 105–9
    conflicts, counselling vs. academic/
       institutional aims 48, 64–3, 105, 108
    financial constraints 45–6, 48–9, 59–60
    generally 10–11
    'hard-to-reach students'/ non attendees
       46–7, 52, 60–2, 71
    new methods/ developments, adoption
       of 50–1, 67–9
    other staff, relationships between 106
    outsourcing, threat of 48–9, 65–6
    risk of harm 51–2, 69–70, 85, 107
    roles, blurring of 106
    service measurement criteria 48, 64–5
    student practical/ welfare issues,
       relationship with 54–6, 72–3, 76–7,
       87–90
    student understanding/ interpretation
       52–3
       cultural influences on 49–50, 66–7
    time constraints/ waiting lists 52–4,
       71–2, 104
children see also safeguarding
    mental health statistics 11
classical conditioning 31
clients see students
cognitive theories 32
    cognitive therapy (CT) 32, 34
    multi-modal therapy (MMT) 34
    rational emotive behavioural therapy
       (REBT) 32–3
cognitive therapy (CT) 32, 34
colleges
    academic framework 18
    counselling service characteristics 5,
       7, 18

community campuses
  academic framework 5–6, 18–19
  counselling service characteristics 5–7, 19
compensation defence mechanisms 35
complaints procedures 92
compulsory counselling
  student responses to 52–3, 72
Confederation of Scottish Counselling
      Agencies (COSCA) 94
confidence issues
  educational success, relevance to 123
  negative school experiences 18, 80
confidentiality 55–6, 66, 102, 105–9
  client records, storage and access 82,
      105, 107–9
  conflicts vs. institutional/ academic aims
      48, 63–5, 105, 108
  and funding 48, 105, 108
  relationships with other staff 102, 106
  and self-harm or suicide 70, 107
  technological developments,
      implications of 67–9
continuing professional development
  for counsellors 91
  general trends 66, 79–80
CORE-OM (Clinical Outcomes in Routine
      Evaluation) 48, 64
Corey, G. 29, 34
costs, of counselling see also funding
  environmental costs 45
  professional costs 45–6
Counselling and Psychotherapy Central
      Awarding Body (CPCAB) 94
counselling experiences see Elaine; Heidi;
      Jane; John; Judy
counselling services, generally
  aims 3, 77, 127–8
counselling theories
  alternative/ creative therapies 41
  behavioural theories 30
    classical and operant conditioning 31
    social learning theory (SLT) 31–2
  cognitive theories 32
    cognitive therapy (CT) 32, 34
    multi-modal therapy (MMT) 34
    rational emotive behavioural therapy
        (REBT) 32–3
  family theories 39
    family adjustment model 40–1
    family dysfunction model 40
    family interaction model 41
    family systems theory 39–40

generally 26
humanistic theories 26
  existential theory 29
  Gestalt theory 30
  person-centred therapy 27
  transactional analysis 28
loss, theories of 39
psychodynamic theories 35
  Adlerian theory 36
  attachment theory 36–7
  integrative theory 37–8
  psychoanalytical theory 35–6
  solution-focused theory 38
counsellors see also trainee counsellors;
      voluntary counsellors
  dual roles 102
  responsibilities 51–2, 70, 102, 106
  risk of harm 51–2, 70
  support mechanisms 70
creative therapies 41
culture, influence on interpretation of
      counselling 49–50, 66–7
data protection 107–8
Dearnley, C. 86
defence mechanisms 35–6
denial 35
depression 85
disability discrimination 110
disempowerment 49
dissociation 36
distance learning
  counselling services 6–7, 20–1
  IT role in 20
  student support needs 86
  trends 20
DNA (did not attend) see non attendance
drop-in counselling services 63
dropping-out
  and counselling continuity/ ongoing
      support 52, 71, 83, 124
  research into 119–20, 124
  and retention, counselling impact on
      120–1, 124
Dryden, W. 32
duty of care see safeguarding
eating disorders 85
eclecticism 38
Egan, G. 38
ego states 28
ELAINE (volunteer counsellor), counselling
      experiences 8–9
  advantages of counselling 8–9

counselling needs and time constraints 53
employment status and continuity 98–9
mature students 53
professional supervision 95–6
Ellis, A. 32–3
email counselling support services 67
emotional abuse 111
Employee Assistance Programmes (EAP) 48–9, 63
employment
    employment concerns, and counselling needs 85
    employment status 97–9
environment
    counselling services setting 82
    influences on counselling services 62–3
equality issues 110
ethical issues
    BACP ethical framework 101
    combined student/ staff counselling services 17, 47–8
    confidentiality 55–6, 66, 82, 105–9
        client records, storage and access 105, 107–9
        conflicts vs. institutional/ academic aims 48, 63–5, 105, 108
        and funding 48, 105, 108
        relationships with other staff 102, 106
        and self-harm or suicide 70, 107
        technological developments, implications of 67–9
    cultural diversity 66–7
    disability discrimination 110
    equality issues 110
    safeguarding 110
        case study 114–15
        definitions 111–13
        regulatory framework 115–16
        responsibilities 113–15
    supervision 7, 103
    and time constraints 104
examinations 22, 31, 39, 85
existential theory 29
exposure therapy 31
failure to thrive 111
family adjustment model 40–1
family dysfunction model 40
family interaction model 41
family systems theory 39–40
family theories 39–41
financing, of counselling services see funding

flexibility
    advantages of 3, 6, 25–6
    cultural variations in attitudes to 66
flooding 31
Freedom of Information 107–8
Freud, S. 35–6
funding, of counselling services
    combined staff/ student services 62–3
    conflicts of interest 46, 48–9, 86–7
    constraints on 45–6, 62–3
    differences between HE and FE 16
    justifications for 48–9
    strategies 59–60
    supplementing, approaches to 45
Further Education (FE)
    difference from HE 15–16
Gallacher, J. 19, 120, 123
Gestalt theory 30
group counselling 9–10, 50, 68, 103
Hall, J.C. 124
Hallett, C. 104
harm, risk of 51–2, 69–70
    codes of practice 111
    self-harm and suicide 11, 51, 70, 85, 107
health, physical, student concerns over 85
HEIDI (student counsellor), counselling experiences 10
    cessation of studies, and continuity of counselling 83
    counsellor's dual roles 102
    employment status and continuity 98
    key student concerns 84–5
    non attendance, dealing with 62, 83
    professional supervision 97
    referrals processes 94
    time constraint issues 52
hierarchy of needs 72–3, 88–9
Higher Education (HE) see also universities
    differences from FE 15–16
    enrolment trends 16
Hodgson, A. 64
holidays, counselling connected with 21–2, 54
Human Resources departments 62–3
humanistic counselling theories 26
    existential theory 29
    Gestalt theory 30
    person-centred therapy 27
    transactional analysis 28
implosion therapy 31
information
    on counselling services 82, 94–5

data protection vs. access 107–8
Freedom of Information 107–8
injury, physical 111
institutional abuse 112
integrative theory 37–8
isolation issues 21
IT
  and alternative approaches to
    counselling 7, 50, 67–9
  as source of student stress 20, 68–9
JANE (FE counsellor), counselling
    experiences
  academic year, influence of nature/
    phases 22
  alternative/ non-verbal therapies 41
  confidentiality 86–7, 106
  conflicts of interest, counselling vs.
    institutional budgets 86–7
  containment issues 49
  counsellor's dual roles 102
  employment status and continuity 99
  impact of counselling 84
  non attendance, dealing with 61
  professional supervision 96
  student's practical/ welfare needs,
    involvement in 55–6, 72–3, 87–90
  students with negative school
    experiences 80
  trainee placements, advantages of 99
JOHN (university counsellor), counselling
    experiences
  attachment issues 37
JUDY (FE counsellor), counselling
    experiences
  group/ personal supervision 103
  negatives/ positives of counselling 8
  student age, influence on non
    attendance 8
Lazarus, A. 34
learning, attitudes to
  adult learners vs. school-age learners
    10–11, 79–81, 123
  and negative school experiences
    18, 80
leaving studies see dropping-out
life goal, notion of 28
loss
  student concerns over 85
  theories of 39
marketing counselling services 82,
  94–5
Maslow, A. 72–3, 88–9

mental wellbeing
  mental health trends in HE students,
    study 127–8
  NUS survey on student mental health
    121–2
  statistics on 11
  student concerns over 85
Miller, G.A. 30
Minuchin, S. 40
'miracle question' 38
motivation 10–11
multi-modal therapy (MMT) 34
National Union of Students (NUS)
  student mental wellbeing survey 121–2
  Think Positive Campaign 4
Naylor, R.A. 119–20
Neenan, M. 32
neglect, physical 111–12
NHS counselling services
  interaction with student counselling
    services 76–7
non attendance
  age, influence on 8
  attitudes to 47, 61–2, 71, 83
    budgetary issues vs. counselling 87
    and compulsory counselling 52–3, 72
    student attitudes 52–3, 72, 87
  average rates, in universities 62
  challenges 46–7, 52, 87
  strategies 60–2, 71
non-verbal therapies 41
Northern Ireland, HE colleges 18
O'Connell, B. 38
online counselling services 7, 50, 67
open learning see distance learning
Open University 20
operant conditioning 31
outreach centres see community campuses
outsourcing, threat of 48–9
  strategies for 65–6
parenting, influence of 8, 103
Pavlov, I. 30
Peris, F. 30
person-centred therapy 27
Piaget, J. 32
Piper, W.E. 81
privacy 82
'problem talk' 38
protected adults, duties and
    responsibilities regarding see
    safeguarding
psychoanalytical theory 35–6

psychodynamic theories 35
    Adlerian theory 36
    attachment theory 36–7
    integrative theory 37–8
    psychoanalytical theory 35–6
    solution-focused theory 38
qualifications, comparison of 139–40
Rana, R. 127–8
rational emotive behavioural therapy
        (REBT) 32–3
rationalisation 35–6
reaction formation 36
Reeves, A. 51, 70
referrals processes 94–5
    compulsory counselling, student
        responses to 52–3, 72
relationships, student concerns over 85
repression 36
retention, counselling service impact on
        120–1, 124, 126–7
risk assessments 92–3
Rogers, C. 27
Ross, W. 33
Royal College of Psychiatrists
    NHS counselling services, interaction
        with student services 76–7
    on student counselling 17
safeguarding 110
    case study 114–15
    definitions 111–13
    regulatory framework 115–16
    responsibilities 113–15
school experiences, negative 18, 80,
        119–20
school leavers 80–1
Scotland, HE reorganisation 18
self-harm 51, 85
    confidentiality issues 70, 107
    trends 11
service measurement criteria 48, 64–5
sexual abuse 111
sexual concerns 85
short-term counselling, effectiveness
        study 126–7
'Silently stressed,' NUS student
        survey 121–2
'Skilled Helper' model 38
Skinner, B.F. 30
Skype counselling services 7, 67–8
Smith, J.P. 119–20
social learning theory (SLT) 31–2
solution-focused theory 38

'solution talk' 38
staff counselling
    combined student/ staff services
        challenges 17, 47–8, 62
        funding 62–3
        management strategies 64
    group counselling 9–10, 50, 68
    institutional attitudes to 63
staffing models 60
stereotypes, avoiding 67
Stewart, I. 28
stigma, studies into 129–30
strategies
    combined student/ staff services 62–4
    for conflicts, counselling vs. academic
        outcomes 64–5
    cultural interpretations of counselling
        66–7
    financial constraints 59–60
    'hard-to-reach students'/ non attendees
        60–2, 71
    new methods/ developments, adoption
        of 67–9
    outsourcing, managing threat of 65–6
    preparedness 67
    risk of harm 69–70
    staffing models 60
    stereotyping, avoiding 67
    time constraints/ waiting lists 71–2
    welfare/ practical issues, relationship
        with 72–3, 76–7
students
    age, influence on counselling 8, 10, 80, 123
    attitudes to counselling
        compulsory counselling 52–3, 72
        cultural influences on 49–50, 66–7
        and different experiences, from
            counsellors 87–90
        and non attendance 47, 52–3, 61–2,
            71–2, 83, 87
        as punishment 52–3, 72
        short-term counselling, effectiveness
            study 126–7
        stigma, study of 129–30
    attitudes to education
        background, relevance of 46
        and negative school experiences 18, 80
        and poor parenting 8, 103
    client/ student types 79–81
    counselling issues 84–6
        academic year, nature/ phases of 21–2,
            54, 130

autonomy 21, 107
being away from home 21, 80–1
isolation 21
practical/ welfare issues 54–6, 72–3,
76–7, 87–90
records, confidentiality vs. access 82,
105, 107–9
time management 21
transitional issues, moving up from
school 21, 85
in FE/HE education
differences from school education 10
support needs, research into 123
information and marketing to 82
and service environment/ setting 82–3
understanding, need for 87–90, 124–5
sublimation 36
suicide
rates 11
risks of 107
supervision 7, 66
cultural influences 66
ethical issues 7, 103
group supervision 50
advantages and disadvantages 9–10,
68, 103
of trainees/ volunteers 71–2, 92, 95–6
systemic desensitisation 31
Tatar, M. 124–5
telephone counselling services 7, 50, 67–8
term-time see academic year
Thyer, B.A. 126
time management 21
counselling challenges 52–4, 71–2
ethical issues 104
waiting lists 52–4, 71–2, 94–5, 104
token economy 31
trainee counsellors
employment status and continuity issues
97–9

placements
host institutions, advantages for 99
restriction issues 72
service funding strategies 60
time constraints, concerns over 52,
71–2
training requirements
professional supervision 71–2, 92,
95–6
risk assessment 92
transactional analysis 28
transitional issues, moving up from school
21, 85
universities
academic framework 4, 16
assessment criteria 16
counselling service characteristics 4–7,
16–17
enrolment trends 4, 16
voluntary counsellors
employment status and continuity
97–9
and funding strategies 59–60
supervision 71–2, 92, 95–6
Vonk, M.E. 126
waiting lists 52–4, 71–2, 94–5, 104
Wallace, P. 128–9
Waller, R. 126–7
welfare concerns, and counselling
needs 85
practical help, role in providing 54–6,
72–3, 76–7, 87–90
Wheeler, S. 92
whistleblowing 106
Wilson, S.B. 120–1
Working Group for the Promotion of
Mental Well-Being in Higher
Education (MWBHE) 3, 77
Yaqoob, T. 4
Yusuf, case study 87–90